My Cup Overflows

A Deeper Study of Psalm 23

Shelly Esser
Marcia Bueschel

 New Hope® Publishers

New Hope Publishers
Birmingham, Alabama

New Hope Publishers
P.O. Box 12065
Birmingham, AL 35202-2065
www.newhopepubl.com

Library of Congress Cataloging-in-Publication Data
Esser, Shelly, 1959-
      My cup overflows : a deeper study of Psalm 23 / by Shelly Esser and Marcia Bueschel.
          p. cm.
      Includes bibliographical references.
      ISBN 1-56309-739-7 (pbk.)
      1. Bible. O.T. Psalms XXIII—Meditations. 2. Christian women—Prayer-books and devotions—English. I. Bueschel, Marcia, 1953- II. Title.

BS1450 23rd .E88 2001
242'.5—dc21

Unless otherwise noted, all Scripture references are from the Holy Bible, New International Version. Copyright © 1973, 1978, 1984 International Bible Society. Used by permission of Zondervan Bible Publishers.

Cover design by Teresa Brooks
Book design by Cheryl Totty

ISBN: 1-56309-739-7

N014124•1001•5M1

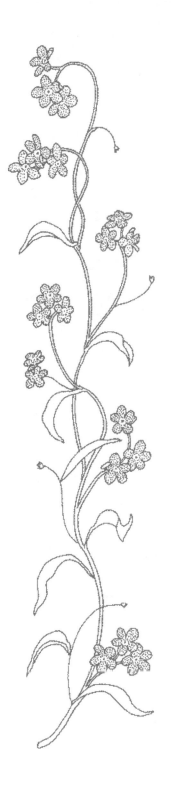

To our husbands, John and Dave, for their faithful love and encouragement.

And to our lambs: Natalie, Megan, Anna, and Stephanie, and Bonnie. May they learn to know the loving guidance of their Shepherd.

Shelly and Marcia

Contents

Introduction

An English actor and a minister were honored at a banquet. In the course of the evening, the actor was requested to give a reading. He chose Psalm 23. He read it in a way that brought out the beauty of the psalm, with clear pronunciation and delicate expression of his art. His friends applauded him. Later that evening, the aged pastor was asked to speak. He too quoted Psalm 23. His voice rang with assurance and was vibrant with love. When he concluded, there was no applause. But there wasn't a dry eye in the room. The actor stepped over to the minister, grasped his hand, and said, "Sir, I know the psalm—but you know the Shepherd" (Olson, 79).

As we embark on the study of Psalm 23, we will ask an important question throughout the study: How well do you know the Shepherd?

There is perhaps no more familiar passage in all of Scripture than Psalm 23. In fact, it is probably one of the best-loved portions in the Bible. Like many other familiar passages, you have probably placed it in memory from childhood, yet it may have no real application to your daily experience. With familiarity, unfortunately, comes great danger: a passage can become meaningless and void of all its rich truths and applications.

As we will see when we dig into this study, there is a great difference between knowing Jesus Christ as Savior and knowing Him as Shepherd—the caretaker and Lord of our lives. It is possible to know Christ as the Savior of our hearts and know nothing of Him as the Shepherd of our lives, as revealed in this psalm. It is all too easy to engage in a superficial, shallow relationship with Christ, while what really awaits each of us is a rich, intimate, daily relationship with Him.

Psalm 23 introduces us to the image of God as the great Shepherd of our lives; a Shepherd who loves us deeply. He invites us to fellowship with Him, to enjoy His presence and rich provisions because we are His own. The Shepherd in Psalm 23 is presented as a personal God, who, because of His great care and concern for our lives, is worthy of all of our trust. By taking a look at how Middle Eastern shepherds care for their sheep, we will be able to more fully understand God's shepherding role in our lives.

Throughout this study, we will learn to carry the presence of the Shepherd into every area of our lives—our relationships, our homes, our jobs, our conflicts, our sorrows, our fears, and our joys. Perhaps you're struggling with a chronically ill child or a difficult work relationship, or maybe your heart has been gripped by some deep sorrow, or maybe you're simply enjoying all of God's goodness and His rich provisions in your life. No matter what the circumstances in our lives, we will discover how the Shepherd's power and presence will see us through every turn. He will be the One walking us through our difficulties with His abiding strength and love. And when we allow the great Shepherd of our hearts to direct and govern our lives, we'll become different people—a different kind of sheep!

Suddenly, we'll begin doing things and living life in ways we'd never have been able to do apart from the Shepherd. As we begin to really follow the Shepherd, we will start to know Him intimately, experiencing all aspects of His personal love and care. He desires to be known and wanted by us, His special sheep.

1

Discovering The Shepherd, My Everything

By Shelly Esser

The Lord is my shepherd,
I shall not be in want.
He makes me lie down in green pastures,
he leads me beside quiet waters,
he restores my soul.
He guides me in paths of righteousness
for his name's sake.

Even though I walk through
the valley of the shadow of death,
I will fear no evil,
for you are with me;
your rod and staff,
they comfort me.

You prepare a table before me
in the presence of my enemies.
You anoint my head with oil;
my cup overflows.
Surely goodness and love will follow me
all the days of my life,
and I will dwell in the house of the Lord
forever.
—Psalm 23

Throughout generations, people have found tremendous comfort and peace in the words of Psalm 23. It has grown to become one of the most familiar and best-loved passages of Scripture. People in every walk and circumstance of life benefit from its truths—the bereaved widow, the unemployed, the depressed, the hurting, as well as those who are thoroughly enjoying a vibrant love relationship with their Shepherd as a result of drinking deeply from all of His rich blessings. They receive the strength, hope, and refreshment needed to carry on amidst the ups and downs of life. When spirits are crushed and bruised, or refreshed and revived, it is to this magnificent Scripture that we most often turn for help and encouragement. Through these short verses we begin to discover our Shepherd in our greatest times of need and joy.

Lord, prepare our hearts today to discover Your continual loving care and concern for every part of our lives, and help us to learn to let You shepherd us as only You can.

Matters for Thought

1. Think of a time when you needed something or someone outside of yourself to help you in a time of great need, a difficult circumstance, a family death, or decisions about a wayward or difficult child. Who or what helped you through this time?

Read Psalm 23 in its entirety.
2. Look closely at David's help in his time of need, as seen throughout this psalm. Where did he find his help and how?

3. Recall the first time you heard or read the psalm. What is an early memory you have of it?

4. Briefly summarize the psalm.

Read Psalms 22 and 24.
5. How do you think these two psalms fit together with Psalm 23?

6. Why do you think these three psalms are known as the Shepherd psalms?

Note: Psalm 23 is part of a trilogy, a group of three psalms (22, 23, 24) that belong together. They present a picture of Christ to us. Psalm 22 speaks of the joy of our salvation, what it means to have a right relationship with Christ; Psalm 23 speaks of being at home with God; and Psalm 24 speaks of what it is going to be like when He comes again.

7. How do these three psalms represent a complete picture of Christ?

8. What does each psalm uniquely tell you about your Shepherd?

9. Why must you know the Shepherd in Psalm 22 before you can come to Psalm 23 and say, "The Lord is my Shepherd?"

10. David, the shepherd/king, has authored the psalm using the imagery of the shepherd/sheep. How is this imagery helpful to you in better understanding your relationship with God?

Notice at verse 5 there is a change in metaphors. It is believed that the psalm contains one metaphor with two aspects. What two roles of the shepherd was David envisioning throughout the psalm?

Verses 1–4

Verses 5–6

How do these two metaphors enhance your picture of Christ as your Shepherd?

11. What verb tense (past, present, or future) is used in every verse?

What does this tell you about God's ministry in your life?

List all the things the Lord is and does, according to the psalm. How do these realities influence your view of God in relationship to your life?

12. As you go through the psalm, how is the presence of the Shepherd carried through each verse?

13. How would the meaning of the psalm change if the Shepherd introduced in verse 1 were not present throughout the entire psalm?

14. From the psalm, what type of relationship with God do you think David had?

15. Make a list of all the things a sheep needs. In what ways have you ever felt like a sheep?

Matters for Reflection

Biblical Imagery
The Lord gave us a lot to think about concerning our relation to the Shepherd and His sheep. Sheep are mentioned 500 times in the Bible, and we are often compared to them throughout Scripture. Once we begin to grasp the depth of our own sheep-like natures, our tendency to be fearful, to wander away, and to make messes of things, we begin to discover how much we need the Shepherd every day, every hour, and every minute of our lives. Think about it. As Christian women, we have someone—the Lord Jesus Christ—who is living in us and for us, and who can help us get through any circumstance or difficulty, living as sheep should!

Discovering the Shepherd as My Everything
It was a hot, humid August day as I boarded the plane. Fresh out of high school, I anticipated spending the next year studying abroad at Capernwray Hall in Northern England. I couldn't wait for the adventure of finally being out on my own.

After tearful goodbyes, I sat on the plane overwhelmed by the aloneness that enveloped me. How would I manage in a foreign country by myself, without my parents who had so lovingly cared for me over the eighteen years? The reality of separation and the unknown unsettled my spirit and began to engulf me with fear. Had I made the right choice in leaving? *Maybe I should have selected a school closer to home*, I thought.

Finally, the long hours of air travel came to a halt and I reached my destination. The school grounds were breathtaking: an old English castle nestled in the rolling hills and lush gardens of England's most beautiful spot, the Lake District. This would be my home for the next year. There, in the magnificent countryside, were the strangest of creatures—flocks of sheep grazing to their hearts' delight. In fact, everywhere I traveled throughout England, there were more sheep! I found myself increasingly fascinated with them. They somehow seemed so content, so oblivious to the rat race around them—they appeared to have no cares or worries, only a complete abandonment in the care of their shepherd.

Against this backdrop, in the hills of England, I began for the first time to experience Christ as the Shepherd of my life. He was no longer hidden in the background, but was fast becoming my everything. I didn't have anyone else to depend on for my continual needs and care, only Christ. He was the one who had faithfully been with me throughout my long and anxious travels. He was the one who had comforted me in my moments of homesickness. He was the one who began to fill my life to overflowing with all His goodness and care. Every step of the way, He was there.

I remember so vividly the day I spent my last English pound—about two American dollars—thinking, "Now what will I do?" The next day, I received a letter from someone I had no recent contact with, with the enclosure of a ten-pound note! There was another time when I finished my last tube of toothpaste. Again, the next morning, not sharing this need with anyone, there on my bed lay a brand-new tube of toothpaste. How could I forget that my Shepherd lovingly met my needs? Several months before I arrived at school, a family that had stayed with us in the States moved three miles down the road from the Bible school, and became my home and family away from home. For the first time in my life and five-year relationship with Him, I experienced very intimately what it meant to have Christ as the Shepherd of my life.

Daily looking upon the lush countryside, I witnessed the earthly shepherds caring for their precious sheep and lambs, just as my Heavenly Father was watching and caring for me—His special, loved sheep!

When I returned to American soil, I was a changed person. Looking back to my time in England, I realized that every single one of my needs had been abundantly met, and it was the Shepherd who had done it! All I needed to do was to let go—to let Him take care of me the way He wanted to. He had always been my Shepherd, but I didn't realize what that aspect of His nature meant. Instead, I filled my days with worry and anxiety. As I've learned to let God be the Shepherd of my life, I have entered into a deeper dimension of my relationship with Him. He has become my everything!

David's Experience with His Shepherd

Like my experience, Psalm 23 is David's personal story of how his Shepherd cared for every detail of his life. It is his testimony to the reality of his God. Because David himself was a shepherd, he thought about how he cared for his own sheep, and realized that God cares for people in just the same way. Just as a shepherd accepts responsibility for every animal in his care, so God cares for every person as though He cares exclusively for that person alone. Just as a shepherd actively cares for his sheep, so God does not watch over our lives passively. He involves Himself in them, to lead and comfort, and to rescue and restore. Just as a shepherd is concerned for his flock, so God is concerned for all of our physical, mental, emotional, and spiritual needs. Everything we experience comes under God's watchful and loving care.

The Message of the Psalm

Psalm 23 is what some commentators have called a "He and Me Psalm." The emphasis is on the fact that there is nothing between a person's soul and God. By the authority of Christ's redemptive work—His death and resurrection—we can trust Him and call Him our personal Shepherd; we can have a relationship with Him. This psalm speaks of following the shepherd today. It speaks of God's ministry in our lives now, not yesterday or tomorrow, but at this moment. May we begin to embrace this great truth about our Heavenly Shepherd, living as different sheep as a result!

Matters for the Heart

1. Can you say as David said, "The Lord is my shepherd?" Why or why not?

Is the Shepherd inside your life right now or outside of it?
In what areas of your life does God need to be your Shepherd?

2. In what area is it most difficult for you to carry the presence of the Shepherd: parenting, a conflict, a job, a marriage relationship, a day-to-day frustration?

3. What difference might it make if you let the Shepherd guide you along?

4. In *My Utmost for His Highest*, Oswald Chambers wrote, "My goal is God Himself, not joy, nor peace, nor even blessing, but Himself, my God." Reflect on that quote. What was he saying?

5. We were created to love the Shepherd with all our hearts, minds, and souls (Deuteronomy 6:5). The greatest thing in life, what gives us the most joy, fulfillment, and contentment, is to love and know our Shepherd intimately. What steps can you take today to nurture your love relationship with your Shepherd?

6. Make a list of God's shepherd care in your life this past week and praise Him for it.

Go through the following exercise in meditation and prayer.
Put your hand up and with each finger representing one word, assign, "The Lord is *my* Shepherd." Hold your fourth finger as you go through the exercise, focusing on "*my*" which is the theme of the entire psalm. This is one of the greatest personal expressions we can ever make about our relationship with Christ.

Now pray. Holding your fourth finger, pray that this truth will become reality in your life in the coming weeks. Pray that the Lord will take on new meaning and application in your life as you get to know Him as your personal Shepherd. Pray about those areas in your life where this is not reality. Pray that your Shepherd will meet you in every moment of need and provide for you. Pray that you will begin to experience the exciting reality of Jesus Christ not only as Savior, but also as the Shepherd and Caretaker of your life.

Matters for Sharing

The focus of this chapter has been to recognize what it means to have the Lord as our personal Shepherd. And just as the Lord so intimately cares for us in every area of our lives, so we can care for the lost or struggling sheep around us in the same way, showing them Christ's love. Try one of these ideas individually or as a group to help someone you know who is experiencing a great need in her life.

• Perhaps you know someone who is really struggling through an illness or a deep disappointment that has led to discouragement. Send her a weekly inspirational card of encouragement pointing her to the help of God in her life and assuring her of your prayers.

• Do you know someone who has recently lost a job or become a single mother? Consider giving an anonymous financial gift to help out with this desperate need. Or think about purchasing a gift certificate to a local grocery store to help with groceries.

• Invite a friend, neighbor, or family member going through a hard time over for dinner and pray with or for her before she leaves. Let her know that you will continue to pray for her and will be available when she needs you.

• Go to your local Christian bookstore and purchase an encouraging gift book filled with appropriate Scripture to encourage someone you know who is really struggling. (There are many beautiful gift books on the market today filled with bite-sized quotations, Bible verses, etc. that can really encourage someone's heart without requiring a lot of reading time.) This would be a great idea for someone who is in the hospital.

2
Discovering the Shepherd, My Source

By Marcia Bueschel

The Lord is my shepherd,
I shall not be in want.
　　　　　　—Psalm 23:1

Have you ever felt like becoming a little child again, curling up in your parent's lap and leaving all the tough questions and decisions to someone bigger than yourself? This psalm of David will help you to feel refreshed in your walk with your Heavenly Father and you will be better equipped to handle the tough times that you face. It is as if we are crawling into the lap of God, finding out who He is, as revealed by David, and where we fit into His plan. As we look at verse one, keep in mind that it establishes the foundation for the remainder of the Psalm.

Lord, thank You for Your love for us and help us to better understand who You are through studying David's words.

Matters for Thought

1. As a small child, what were some of your needs?

2. As you were growing up, what did your parent(s) provide for you?

3. List some things you feel you need now. Include physical, emotional, social, and spiritual needs in your list.

Read Psalm 23, then go back and reread verse one.
4. When you hear the term "the Lord," what do you think of?

5. In the preface of your Bible, see if there is an explanation of how "LORD" is spelled. There are three different spellings—"lord," "Lord," and "LORD." Try to find out what the different meanings are for each word, and then check to see which word David uses.

6. Think of the different relationships that you have. What picture or image would you choose to describe how you see God? Why?

7. David speaks of the LORD being his Shepherd. What do you think a shepherd does?

8. David identifies himself with sheep. Throughout Scripture sheep sometimes represent you and me. To help you identify sheep behavior, look up the following verses and relate them to yourself:

Psalm 119:176
Isaiah 53:6
Matthew 9:36
Luke 15:3–7
John 10:3,27

9. Do you know if you are a lost sheep or a found sheep? Check the *Steps to Leading a Person to Christ* at the back of this book for further help.

David felt great security in his Shepherd. That same security is also available to us. We have the benefit of living after Christ's life, death, and resurrection; and through the New Testament, we have a far greater knowledge of who the "LORD" is.

Read John 10:1–16.

10. This passage has much to say about Jesus, the Good Shepherd. List some of His attributes.

11. What privileges and blessings are listed for the sheep who are part of His fold?

12. **Reread John 10:4–5.** What can we understand about our Shepherd from this passage?

13. C. W. Slemming, in his book *He Leadeth Me*, explains that a Middle Eastern sheepfold is a low walled enclosure with no door, just an opening for the sheep to pass through. The shepherd (or shepherds, if more than one flock is present) stands in the opening as his sheep are passing through. He is then able to look over each sheep and check for illness or injuries. He also can check to see that each sheep is present and not lost.

Look at John 10:7–10.

a. How is Jesus the door for His sheep? (In some translations this reads "gate.")

b. What promise is listed here?

14. Look over the following quote by Phillip Keller from *A Shepherd Looks at Psalm 23:*

In memory I can still see one of the sheep ranches in our district which was operated by a tenant sheepman. He ought never to have been allowed to keep sheep. His stock were always thin, weak, and riddled with disease and parasites. Again and again they would come and stand at the fence staring blankly through the woven wire at the green lush pastures which my flock enjoyed. Had they been able to speak I am sure they would have said, "Oh, to be set free from this awful owner!"

Now look again at verses 11–13.
a. How does the character of the shepherd affect the flock?

b. Try to relate this to the relationships you have. Who are you shepherding (leading or influencing)?

Both Peter and Paul identified the early Christian elders as shepherds responsible for the care of God's flock. **Read Acts 20:28 and 1 Peter 5:1–4.**

15. Identify some shepherds that you know (i.e. pastors, teachers, ministry leaders). What are the characteristics of good and bad shepherds?

16. How can the example of shepherds be used in developing the leadership within your church or small group?

17. What aspect of a shepherd can you most identify with, such as watching over those you love or guiding your children?

18. What aspect would you like to see grow in your life?

19. David says that he "shall not want" or lack anything. Consider the difference between needs and wants. In what practical ways do you see God meeting your needs?

20. Think of some wants that He may be blessing you with, as well.

Matters for Reflection

My Shepherd's Touch

I spent four years in the Navy. During the first three years, I was spiritually lacking. Though I had accepted Jesus as my Savior in high school, and had peace about my eternal destination, I had yet to make Him Lord of my life. There was no external difference between my actions and those of others around me. I know my parents spent years praying for me, and one day when I found myself feeling really lost, Mom reminded me (again) that Christ wanted to be Lord in my life.

It finally clicked. I had been looking at those around me and getting my cues for acceptance from the popular magazines, believing that even though the Bible was the Word of God, it was terribly outdated and had nothing relevant to say to me personally. For the first time, I looked at myself and my world through eyes opened by the Spirit of God. I realized then how much God loved me as I was, and how much I needed a Shepherd to watch over me every day, and to take care of me and make me into a fluffy, contented, obedient sheep. Slowly, my values, actions, and goals in life started to reflect the inner change that had taken place. Do I sometimes still insist on my own way? Of course. You see, I'm still a sheep!

Many of us have areas in our lives with which we struggle. For me, it has been my husband's frequent unemployment periods. I often wonder if the Lord really does have my best interest in mind. As Dave was laid off because company after company reduced its engineering staff, I've been forced to work more hours outside the home. This hasn't been my choice; I'd prefer to stay home with our daughter. But for reasons unknown to me, Dave has been the one to be home with Bonnie during the summers. He's been at my side to see her off to her first day of school. He's been able to attend her school plays, and been available to do lots of things with her that other dads have not.

At times, I almost became jealous, but I needed to remind myself that these were special times in their relationship and, as a family, we were all doing what needed to be done to get by. It's interesting that each time Dave started a new job, there was some aspect that was better than the previous one. He is the kind of person who will stay at a job even if he doesn't like it. I believe the Lord knows that the only way to move Dave on is by forcing him to leave.

Did the Lord provide us with all of our needs? The mortgage and bills somehow got paid and we had food on the table. However, it took a while to realize that I could trust Him with these things. The first layoff was difficult for all of us. But by the fifth one, we knew that the Lord is faithful and would take care of us. Only He knows the lessons that will be the best teachers in our lives. The question is, can we learn to be content while He provides us with our needs, or are we always expecting to have our wish lists filled too?

A Sheep's Nature

There is a big difference between a flock of sheep that has been lovingly attended to by a caring shepherd, and a flock that is ill-kept by an uncaring hired hand. Sheep can struggle, starve, and suffer one hardship after another, or they can be well fed, free of pests, and very contented. It depends on what kind of shepherd they have.

Sheep do not do well on their own. They require more attention and care than any other type of livestock. They are fearful, timid, stubborn, and their herd instinct, or their "flock folly," as Stuart Briscoe calls it in *What Works When Life Doesn't*, can get them into endless trouble. They have no natural defenses—no quills, no fangs or claws, no venom, and no "skunky" scent. They lack a sense of direction. If they become lost they won't find their way home like Rover would. It is apparent that sheep need someone to care for them.

Phillip Keller writes, "The behavior of sheep and people is similar in many ways. Yet, despite these characteristics, Christ chooses us, buys us, calls us by name, makes us His own and delights in caring for us."

The Shepherd's Nature

One of the jobs of a shepherd is to "earmark" his sheep, something that functions like a brand. When Keller was a shepherd, he used a knife to notch a special feature on the ear. It was painful not only for the sheep, but also for that loving shepherd to do. But by doing so, it was possible to tell, even from a distance, which sheep were his.

From the realms of heaven the Lord knows which of us carry the mark of the Cross, the blood of the Lamb. That mark identifies us as belonging to Christ for all time. It was painful for Him to die on that Cross. Likewise, it's painful for us to admit we need a shepherd to care for us. But both steps are necessary if we are to be part of the Lord's heavenly flock. Our Christianity is more than just wearing a cross around our necks. Is Christ real in our lives; is He Lord of our thoughts, actions and deeds? Are we different from the people around us? Or do we blend into our surroundings like chameleons? Some of us are gifted to be bold evangelists. Others have quieter gifts, so that in many ways we do look like others around us. But if someone were to study our lives—how we spend our money, what our priorities are, how we make decisions, what our values are—would they find us different from the norm? If so, what could they attribute that difference to?

In *I Shall Not Want*, Robert Ketcham tells this story: A girl in Sunday School, along with the rest of her class, was asked to recite Psalm 23. She got up in front of her class and stated, "The Lord is my shepherd. That's all I want." Is that reality in your own heart?

Spend some time in prayer now, either individually, as pairs, or in a small group.

Matters for the Heart

1. Thank the Lord for all He provides for you. Make a written list to help you dwell on these blessings.
2. Thank the Lord for providing Jesus as your Shepherd.
3. Thank Him for His Word and for the Holy Spirit, who helps you understand it.
4. Ask Him to help you become a better shepherd of the flock He has entrusted to you.
5. Thank Him that Jesus understands you better than you understand yourself, and loves you deeply.
6. In silent prayer, let Him know your deepest needs and desires. He knows them all anyway, but this helps you become more aware of these concerns.

Matters for Sharing

Since the focus of this chapter has been on how the Shepherd meets our deepest needs and sometimes gives us our wants as well, consider how you might be His hands in meeting someone's needs around you.

• Is there someone you know who has a physical need you can help fill—a young mom in the neighborhood who might love a few hours of free babysitting, or an elderly friend or relative who might appreciate a ride to the store or a lunch date?

• Is there a holiday coming that you could invite someone to join who you might otherwise be lonely? By doing so, you might be meeting an emotional or social need.

• There are many missions agencies who accept donations so that Bibles might be placed in hands that would otherwise be without one. Consider a donation to such a worthy cause. Along similar lines, many churches have libraries that would love your extra study materials and books.

• Do you know someone who would love to have a Bible with references or commentaries? There are many on the market that speak to different situations. Bless someone with a special Bible just for them.

3

Discovering the Shepherd, My Nourishment and Refreshment

by Shelly Esser

He makes me lie down in green pastures,
he leads me beside quiet waters.
—Psalm 23:2

We are living in a day of extreme pressures, busyness, and overall weariness. Everything about us is tired and exhausted. Our minds are tired. Our bodies are tired. Our spirits are tired. Many of us find ourselves running from one event to the next in a whirlwind of activity: carpools, children's activities, volunteer work, careers, church service, not to mention just the day-to-day activities necessary to maintain life. After a while this kind of fast-paced lifestyle begins to take a very heavy toll on us, especially in our relationship with God.

It is here that Christ comes, offering Himself to us as a Shepherd who is able to lead each one of us into green pastures and quiet places where we can lie down and rest from all the rush and burdens of life. Our Shepherd leads us to places where we can recapture what rest and refreshment is all about, offering us lasting peace and teaching us how He alone satisfies His sheep.

Lord, help us to follow Your leading so we can find the nourishment and refreshment that our weary souls so desperately need today. Remind us that no matter what burdens we carry, we can experience a deep, lasting peace in the middle of them, because You are our ever-present Shepherd.

Matters for Thought

1. Review the various activities in your life right now. Do you find yourself doing more and enjoying it less?

2. Corrie ten Boom once said, "Beware of the barrenness of a busy life." How does busyness lead to spiritual barrenness?

3. In what area of your life do you need to experience more rest and peace today—where are you weary and exhausted?

Read Psalm 23:2 out loud.

4. To what two places does the Lord take His sheep in verse 2?

a. What is the significance of these places?

b. How do these places provide refreshment for your life, personally?

5. Verse 2 mentions "green pastures" which represent the Word of God, and "still waters" which represent peace and refreshment. Why do you think the verse comes right after verse 1 and before the following four verses?

6. What pronoun does David use in this verse? How is it evidenced here that the Shepherd cares for your needs?

a. Who is the focus of the verse?

b. Why is that focus so important?

7. If we're going to experience true rest and "lie down," why must we first be at peace?

8. Scripture speaks of two kinds of peace. **Look up Romans 5:1 and Philippians 4:7.**

a. What is the difference between "peace with God" spoken of in Romans and the "peace of God" spoken of in Philippians?

b. Which peace do you think Psalm 23:2 most closely speaks of?

9. **Look up Mark 1:35, Luke 4:42, Luke 6:12 and John 5:19.** From these verses, what can you conclude about Jesus' "pasture" experience? What do you notice about His feeding pattern?

10. What is the Word of God able to accomplish in your life according to the following verses?

Psalm 37:31
Psalm 119:11, 28, 98, 105, 130
John 15:3
Acts 20:32
2 Timothy 3:16
James 1:21

11. Water, in Scripture, frequently symbolizes God's blessings and spiritual refreshment. To drink spiritually means to "take in," "accept," or "believe." Where are you in need of a spiritual drink?

12. Some scholars suggest that the word *still* is in the past tense in the original, and the text should read, "He leads me beside the stilled waters." When you face the raging waters of sorrow, affliction, heartbreak, heartache, and disappointments that often keep you from rest and peace, how does the truth that your Shepherd moves in and stills the waters around you bring comfort and peace?

13. Notice the verbs *makes* and *leads* used in this verse. How do they imply that the sheep have to be willing to cooperate with their Shepherd? What is required of us?

14. Why are spiritual rest and refreshment so vital for our growth and well-being?

Matters for Reflection

Discovering the Shepherd, My Nourishment

I was frantically typing at my computer, trying to wade my way through the tasks I had over-committed myself into, when my two-year-old appeared at the door. "Mommy, can I please have a drink of water?"

"Just a minute, honey," I replied.

About a half an hour later, she emerged again, "Mommy, can I please have a drink of water?"

"In a minute, in a minute!"

Again, a block of time swept by before she appeared at the office door, this time, raising her little voice, "Mommy, can I please have a drink of water, now?!"

Two hours and three visits later, I had finally heard her loud and clear, but I found myself agitated and irritated at her request. After all, I had all of these deadlines approaching, and I had to get these projects done today! My heart was so full of anxiety and weariness with that a seemingly simple request for water required a monumental effort.

As I went upstairs to fill her tippy cup with water, my Shepherd whispered to me, "Natalie's not the only one you've been saying 'just a minute to.' You've been putting off time alone with me for weeks and as a result you're frazzled and coming apart." My daughter wasn't the only one who needed a cup of refreshing water.

I, too, needed the refreshing touch of my Shepherd, not just now and then but regularly, if I was to be effective in my mothering and the other things God was calling me to do.

I was having an increasingly difficult time managing my family and commitments as it was. How in the world was I going to manage in a few weeks with another baby in the picture? Some drastic changes were going to have to take place. Some "house-cleaning" was in order. I had to let the Shepherd houseclean my priorities so I could develop a regular "feeding pattern" in the green pastures of His Word.

So often it's hard to make ourselves lie down and leave our lives to our Shepherd, isn't it? But as David points out in verse two, the first step to experiencing the Lord's abundant provisions of nourishment and refreshment in our lives is to "lie down." It's to cooperate with Him; to cooperate with His plan and leading, His priorities for our lives. We want to be "doing" instead of lying down. We do not realize that it is the lying down, the going beside the "still waters" that will give us the energy for the "doing," not the other way around.

When sheep are seen lying down in pasturelands, it means their tummies are full. They are completely content and satisfied. So often, we long to experience the Shepherd's rest and peace in our lives, but we've missed the most vital preliminary step—first letting His Word nourish our weary souls. It is only then that we can lie down from the hectic pace around us, finding the rest and refreshment we so desperately need, and getting refueled and renewed to face the changes and challenges of life.

The place of rest David describes for us here in this verse is a place of rich, lush pastureland with an abundance of tender grass. What a beautiful picture of God's Word. It's a metaphor for all that makes life flourish.

The Word of God is one of the Shepherd's primary means of guidance in our lives. Once we begin to know His Word, letting it nourish our hearts, we're going to know the things He desires us to be involved with, and the things that will energize us, not deplete us. When we begin to know our Bibles, the Shepherd touches us with the peace and rest we so often long for. Knowing the Word gives us the promises needed to free us from fearfulness, restlessness, and worry. Regularly feeding on the abundant "green pastures" of God's Word brings us lasting peace and rest. As we get to know the Word, the greater grows our intimacy with our Shepherd.

While in college, I was part of a Christian group on campus that encouraged students to disciple each other. I was discipled by a student who showed me the importance of spending regular time with God in His Word. She helped me develop a regular feeding pattern in my life that has stuck with me to this day. Over the years, however, there have been those times of busyness, when I have settled for only a couple of blades of grass or no grass at all, and inevitably at those times I have found my heart filled with anxiety, especially when facing daily burdens. I have noticed, without fail, that when I am regularly in the Word, no matter what happens in my life, I experience a "peace that surpasses all understanding." I have a deep sense of my Shepherd's presence and that He is in control of every detail of my life, leading me in right paths.

Discovering the Shepherd, My Refreshment

A Middle Eastern shepherd touches each one of his sheep daily, and if for some reason he misses one, that one doesn't hear his song later when he calls it. Likewise, we need to let our Heavenly Shepherd touch us daily through His Word. Otherwise, we're not going to hear Him speaking to us throughout the day. Because I had become so over-committed, I didn't have time to be in God's Word (or so I thought). As a result, my life became one big knot of anxiety. This was certainly not the picture of rest! Sadly, I neglected my daughter's simple request for a drink, just as I had been neglecting the very thing that would fill my inner spirit. We need to establish a stable feeding pattern if we're going to develop an intimate relationship with the Shepherd, and if we're going to please Him. Part of being the kind of sheep the Shepherd desires us to be is having those times of spiritual nourishment and refreshment.

My daughter, Natalie, wasn't the only one who needed water that frazzled day. I, too, realized just how barren my life had become, learning finally to say "Just a minute" to the activities in my life, instead of to my Shepherd. God used my toddler that day to get my attention, to show me just how spiritually malnourished I had become, and to point me to the "green pastures" and "still waters" my Shepherd had waiting for me. Out of the mouths of babes!

Matters for the Heart

1. In what ways does the Shepherd feed you? What kinds of pastures does He take you to? What are you feeding on now?

2. Have you established a regular "feeding pattern"? If not, set some goals for yourself. Have a plan, a place and a time of day, a book or passage of the Bible to begin with, and start nourishing your weary heart in God's Word. (To help you get started, there are all kinds of excellent 'read-through the Bible' plans, as well as devotionals, available at Christian bookstores.)

3. Recall a time when God's Word brought refreshment and peace to your heart. Where do you need His Word to nourish your life today—in a troubled relationship, an unexpected circumstance, a heartache, a fear, a financial worry? Ask God to reveal His Shepherd heart to you through His Word.

4. What indications (attitudes, behaviors, etc.) do you have in your life that remind you when you haven't been feeding regularly in the "green pastures" of His Word?
5. David talked about the Lord leading him.

a. How are you allowing the Lord to work in your life, following His lead and choices for you? How does His Word lead you?

b. What has He led you to do this past week? What makes it hard for you to follow?

c. What difference does it make in your spiritual growth when you follow? When you don't? Share an example.

6. Make a fresh commitment today to take time away from your hectic lifestyle to spend with your Shepherd in spiritual nourishment and refreshment. Take time to be still, sitting at His feet. Meditate on and memorize Psalm 46:10, which says, "Be still, and know that I am God."

Matters for Sharing

This chapter reminds us that our Shepherd offers us places of rest throughout the whirlwind of activity that defines many of our lives. Think about how you or your group might provide rest and refreshment to someone you know who needs it.

• Today many families are living in what has become known as the "sandwich generation," where they are caring for both their children and their aging parents. Do you know someone in this situation? How might you give them a rest in the midst of the demands? To lighten their load, find a couple of other women to take turns delivering home-cooked meals in disposable containers or offer to relieve them from their duties so they can attend a special event or run out to get a haircut. Provide them with mini-getaways. Look for needs and just meet them.

• Stress is one of the first signs that our lives are overloaded. For many women, like single moms, the overload is not a choice—it's a way of life. Would you have a few hours every other week to lend a single mom who needs a break? Perhaps you could clean her house so she can go out and do something for herself, or do her laundry so she can read a book or have lunch with a friend.

• The fast pace of everyday life often takes its toll on marriages. Do you know a couple who is greatly suffering in their marriage and who could use some time away from it all to focus on getting their marriage back on track? Offer to watch a couple's children so they can have a weekend getaway to refresh their marriage. Many couples have no close relatives to help out in this way. This will be a very practical way for you to model Christian love.

• Working women are juggling more and more responsibilities. With long hours at work and running their households at home, there are often not enough hours in the day to get everything done. Do you know a working mom who is in need of some rest? Offer to take over a meal one night so she doesn't have to cook when she comes in from a busy day, or pick up some groceries for her next time you go to the store so she doesn't have to. Include a ribbon with a relevant Scripture verse tied to it with the meal or groceries, reminding her that God cares about all of her needs.

4
Discovering the Shepherd, My Restorer and Guide

By Marcia Bueschel

He restores my soul.
He guides me in paths of righteousness
for his name's sake.
                              —Psalm 23:3

Several questions come to mind when looking at Psalm 23:3. What is a soul? Why did David's soul need restoring? Where do "paths of righteousness" fit in? What does this have to do with sheep? These are the issues we'll be addressing in this chapter.

I love the Psalms because they speak not only of joys, but also of sorrows. David was known as the "man after God's own heart." He was a not just a shepherd, eventually becoming a king, but also a poet. He had the ability to express his deepest emotions—from the heights of praise to the depths of despair.

Perhaps you can relate to his feelings. Just because we are believers does not mean we will float carefree through life. Our loving Lord created us as emotional beings. He knows us better than we know ourselves. We aren't surprising Him when we come to Him with heavy hearts—He already knows what is there! He can be our restorer, if we let Him.

Lord, thank You for David's example of honesty and for these words of Scripture. Help us, today, to relate to these words.

Matters for Thought

He Restores Me

1. Make a list of emotions that you have felt in the past week.

2. Which ones are you feeling now?

3. What are some different ways that people handle their emotions? For instance, how do you handle happiness? Sadness?

4. What is the difference between sadness, depression, and despair?

5. Recall the last time you felt sad or despairing. Who or what helped you?

Read Psalm 23, then go back and reread verse 3.
6. According this verse, who is the one that restores David's soul?

7. According to Zondervan's Bible Dictionary, a soul is "the non-material ego of man in its ordinary relationships with earthly and physical things." It's our non-physical self, and includes our minds, wills, hearts, and spiritual natures. Speculate why David's soul needed restoring. For one reason, it may help to briefly review the story of his affair with Bathsheba. This can be found in 2 Samuel 11:1 to 12:13.

8. What are some reasons our souls may need restoring?

9. According to the Random House dictionary, one of the definitions of *restore* is "to bring back health, soundness or vigor." The Lord can work in our lives through His Word, His Spirit within us, and our circumstances, which include others around us.

How can:
a. the Bible restore our souls?

b. the Holy Spirit restore our souls?

c. God use our circumstances to restore our souls?

10. How can we be of comfort to others? Look up the following verses for some hints:

2 Corinthians 1:3–7
Galatians 6:2
Romans 12:15 and 15:1
Ephesians 4:26

Psalm 42:11 speaks of David's soul being cast down. Once again, this is "sheep" language. One of the definitions for *cast* relates to an animal who is on its back and can't turn onto its feet again. According to Phillip Keller, even the most healthy, fluffy sheep can become cast. If they lie down in a slight hollow, stretch out to get comfy, and roll onto their backs, their centers of gravity shift and they can't get their legs under themselves. If they get a little frantic and start to kick, they only succeed in tiring themselves out. Within a few hours they may die if they are not rescued.

Do you ever feel like a cast down sheep, lying flat on your back, floundering away and not being able to get back on your feet? A shepherd keeps watch over his sheep so that if one becomes cast he can gently put it back onto its feet, massage its legs to help the circulation, and restore it. Jesus, our Good Shepherd, can restore us when we are cast down, and He does so with kindness and gentleness.

He Guides Me
David puts restoring his soul side-by-side with being lead down "paths of righteousness for His name's sake." We are aware that at one point in his life, David very much followed his own path, even though he knew it was wrong. That path led to Bathsheba. Eventually he had her husband murdered to cover his tracks. Psalm 51:12, "Restore to me the joy of your salvation and grant me a willing spirit, to sustain me," is David's cry for help to his Holy God, begging that the joy of his salvation would once again be returned to him.

David knew his soul needed restoring. He had not followed the Lord's leading down paths of righteousness, but deliberately did something he knew was wrong. David could have allowed his failures in life to drive him further from God, but he didn't. Instead, he chose to acknowledge those failures to God and seek restoration.

11. How do we know if we're on the right path when it comes to decision-making?

12. Why do you think the Lord cares which paths we follow?

13. What do you think this has to do with His name?

Matters for Reflection

Restoring Our Souls

How does the Good Shepherd restore our souls? David was aware that his soul needed restoring. This is an important point, for I believe that many people are unaware of their emotional lives. How can you seek to have your soul restored if you don't know that it needs restoring? For example, if you were brought up in a home where sadness, fear, or worries were not acknowledged, you learned at a very early age that these were "no-no's," you probably suppressed your feelings. Now, as an adult, you may not be aware that you have times of feeling blue.

I've learned that God gave us all of our emotions, such as sadness, gladness, anger, fear, hurt, and shame. Emotions are neither good nor bad. They simply *are*. It's how we choose to handle them that makes the difference. Do we acknowledge them and work through them, or do we ignore them? Do we control our emotions, or do they control us? Do we react to situations, or do we respond to them?

We need to take the first step—to be aware that our souls may need restoring. Some of us may need to ask God to help us become more in touch with our emotions. The first step may be to tell God that you are experiencing a particular emotion (sadness, for example) and to ask Him to help you uncover why you're feeling that way. The next step may be to ask God what you need to do with that emotion. Is there some healing action that needs to take place? This may take time, may involve grief and tears, may involve forgiving someone. You may need outside help or counsel. Perhaps you need to become willing to let go of something that is troubling you. Ultimately, if you trust the Shepherd, you will find your soul restored.

Remember that God works through His Word, the Bible, His Spirit—that still, small voice within believers—and our circumstances.

A Time for Restoration
Several years ago, Dad was diagnosed with Parkinson's disease and was placed on medication. He became very "weepy," not like himself at all. I was certain he was dealing with depression. Granted, some of his behavioral changes could have been related to his medication, but I felt that there were deeper issues involved.

We all vacationed together during the summer, so I had some lengthy private time with him. I discovered he had some grave misconceptions about his disease. We were able to talk openly and freely about some of his fears and concerns. I saw the expression on his face change as relief came and fears subsided. Here was a man who was afraid to speak of his greatest anxieties, so they came out in other ways. Until he found a safe place to talk, a listening ear, and some misconceptions put aright, he was miserable.

Perhaps you have had a similar experience when someone has helped you or you have been a help to others. If so, this is a small example of how we can be the Lord's instruments in restoring others' souls.

My own sense of restoration has come about just recently. My dear, sweet grandmother died two weeks ago. She's the person I "take after," and we were pretty close. I'm sad, and I miss her, but I'm so thankful that she had a close relationship with the Lord. She was eagerly waiting to see Him face to face. She was also blessed because she died the way she hoped she would. When I have the urge to give her a call and realize I can't anymore, the Lord has truly been my comfort, gently reminding me that she's talking to Him now.

The Paths We Choose

What about the paths we choose to follow in life? Do you know that sheep are creatures of habit? They will graze in the same pasture until there is nothing left but bare soil. They will follow the same path over and over again until there is a deep rut and the land erodes away. If the sheep were left to follow their own way, they would soon be surrounded by lifelessness. Because of their herd instinct, sheep will also blindly follow each other.

How many of us, in our shepherding role as parents, have heard the familiar lament from our kids, "But everyone else is going!" Because we love them, we may have refused permission to go along with the crowd, basing our decision on knowledge our children may not possess. A good shepherd keeps his flock on the right paths. He doesn't lead them astray. He also keeps his sheep on the move from one pasture to another so that there is good grazing ahead. He knows where he is leading them and has a definite plan in mind.

We, as sheep, cannot see into the future. We do not know the dangers that lie there, nor can we see the opportunities and rewards. Our job is to follow the Shepherd and trust in His care.

Matters for the Heart

1. Think of an area where you need God's leading. Use the following as a prayer:

Lead, kindly Light, amid the encircling gloom,
   Lead Thou me on!
The night is dark and I am far from home:
   Lead Thou me on!
Keep Thou my feet; I do not ask to see
The distant scene; one step enough for me.
—John Henry Newman, From *Pillar of the Cloud*

2. Pray with a partner, sharing one area where you need the Lord's loving restoration and one area where you are seeking His guidance. Take a few minutes and pray for each other. Thank Him for His loving care.

3. During the next week, commit this verse to memory: "In all your ways acknowledge him, and he will make your paths straight."
—Proverbs 3:6

The Lord is our Restorer and Guide, if we will look to Him. We can tell Him our deepest sorrows and He understands. Consider how you can be His ears for those around you in need.

Matters for Sharing

• Have you ever just needed someone to talk to? Perhaps there are people around you who need a listening ear. Are you available? Remember, the best listeners are those who can keep their ears open and their mouths shut! Try not to give advice unless asked.

• Commit to pray for someone—your child, your spouse, your best friend. Ask them for specific prayer requests.

• Find a prayer partner whom you can pray for and who will pray for you. Set up a regular time to meet on the phone or for coffee. It is a comfort knowing that someone you care for is praying for you. Remember that prayer requests should stay confidential! Don't share the information with anyone.

• For those you know who are deeply troubled, do you know of a Christian counselor or therapist you might refer them to? Some churches have lay counselors. Perhaps this is an area you are gifted in and could become involved in so you can minister to those who are hurting.

5

Discovering The Shepherd, My Companion and Comforter

By Shelly Esser

Even though I walk through
the valley of the shadow of death,
I will fear no evil,
for you are with me;
your rod and staff,
they comfort me.
—Psalm 23:4

Life is hard. Illness. Tragedy. Poverty. Broken dreams. Divorce. Single parenting. Strained relationships. Miscarriage. Infertility. A handicapped child. Discouragement. Depression. Loneliness. Death. Into these dark places of our lives the Shepherd comes, promising us His presence and comfort. David, at this halfway point in the psalm, introduces us to the intimate nature of our Shepherd. The psalm turns here to address the Shepherd directly—it's face-to-face communication, a relationship at its deepest level.

Have you ever noticed that often, when things are going well in our lives, we can be content to talk *about* the Lord; but when the sky darkens, we want to deal with Him *directly*. We want to feel His presence. Such is the conversation here. Verse 4 takes on the most intimate discourse and affection possible.

There is probably no greater time in our life to experience the intimate care of Christ than when we walk through the dark valleys of our lives. We will never travel alone. The Shepherd is always with us. He is completely reliable and trustworthy. He will be there with us, not ahead of us as we've seen earlier in the psalm, but right alongside us to escort us through, every step of the way.

Lord, remind me today that I am never alone, as I go through the dark valleys of my life. Thank You for the truth that "You are with me." My valley may well be full of shadows, but thank You that Your presence overshadows them all. Comfort my heart today as I face the darkness and hold me close, calming my every fear.

Matters for Thought

1. What circumstances in your life most often cause you to experience fear?

2. What do you find to be the most helpful for "walking through" the valleys in your life?

Read Psalm 23:1–4 in several different versions, twice.
3. Examine the language of the first three verses carefully, and compare them to verse 4. What changes do you notice?

4. To whom does David now speak directly? What do you think this change indicates and why is it so important?

5. What do the words "even though" imply?

6. **Look up James 1:2 and John 16:33.** How do these verses help you understand that phrase?

7. a. What do you think the "valley of the shadow of death" refers to?

b. What does the "valley of the shadow of death" represent in your life today?

8. How can the Shepherd's presence make the difference when sorrow, adversity, bereavement, disappointment, and rejection break into your life?

9. Study the word *through*. Look it up in a dictionary. How does the inclusion of the word *through* bring you comfort when facing life's shadows?

10. Fear is one of the greatest enemies of sheep.
a. How can "fear" keep you from experiencing the Shepherd's presence in the valleys of life?

b. **Read 1 John 4:18–19 and Isaiah 41:10.** What can you learn about fear from these verses? What is the role of our Shepherd in these verses?

11. **Look up Isaiah 43:1–3.**
a. What do these verses guarantee for believers when valleys of sorrow and hardship come into their lives?

b. Notice the pronouns used in this passage. What does this passage say about "walking through?"

c. How does the passage reinforce the message of Psalm 23:4?

12. **Read Hebrews 13:5–6.** Why is this promise so important to remember in the "valleys" of your life? How does it reinforce the phrase "for you are with me?"

13. The second half of the verse speaks of the Shepherd's rod, which is an instrument of discipline, and the staff, which is an instrument of guidance and protection for the sheep. In what ways do the Shepherd's rod and staff provide comfort for our lives?

14. What does it mean to "comfort?" In what ways has the Shepherd comforted you in your "valley" experiences?

15. Look up the word *comfort* in a Bible concordance. Find three verses you think help explain "comfort" and write the verses in your own words. What do you notice about the verses?

16. **Read 2 Corinthians 1:3–4.** What do these verses tell you about comfort? What is your wonderful responsibility and opportunity to do once you are comforted?

Matters for Reflection

Discovering the Shepherd, My Companion

It was a beautiful, warm summer day and I had just returned home from getting my hair cut. I heard the phone ring as I stepped in the door. I raced upstairs to see who it was. I found my husband with his face buried in his hands, clutching the phone. I asked who it was. With a despairing look I will never forget, his eyes met mine as he choked out the shocking news: his parents had been killed in a car accident on their way to an out-of-state class reunion.

I couldn't believe it! How could this be happening? We had just moved back to the area after a long absence to begin full-time ministry in a local church, where my husband was to be the new associate pastor. We were so looking forward to being near both of our parents and our new daughter's grandparents. This isn't how it's supposed to be. It's so brutally unfair. "Lord, how are we going to get through this?" I cried.

In a state of shock and despair, we somehow made it through the funeral and unbearably long days afterward. But I was shattered. Tragedy had destroyed the neatly arranged pattern of everything I had hoped for. I felt lost, alone, powerless, and abandoned. My faith was being stretched to the breaking point.

Slowly, life began to regain some normalcy until my grandfather died two months later. My already broken heart swelled even more as one more time we said goodbye to a loved one.

Looking back on those dark days, I often ask myself the question, "How did I make it through?" I know. My Shepherd carried me "through" every step of the way. It was His abiding, constant presence that kept me going. He is the One who made it possible for me to get up every morning to face another difficult day, filled with painful reminders. As I learned to rely on Him, putting my weak hands in His strong ones, He gave me the necessary resources to do what had to be done, no matter how difficult it was. His strength gave me the supernatural ability to make it "through."

Discovering the Shepherd, My Comforter

His Word was an integral part of not only comforting me during that time, but of providing me with all that I needed. Verses that I learned over the years like, "The Lord is close to the brokenhearted and saves those who are crushed in spirit" (Psalm 34:18); and "Come to me, all you who are weary and burdened, and I will give you rest" (Matthew 11:28); and "The peace of God, which transcends all understanding, will guard your hearts and your minds in Christ Jesus" (Philippians 4:7), to name a few, became my lifeline "through" the valley.

If we're not daily coming to the "green pastures" of God's Word (as we learned in chapter 3) and feeding there, when the crisis and dark experiences strike our lives we will have nothing from which to draw. There were days, even weeks, when I couldn't read my Bible or pray other than, "Lord, help me get through another day," because my heart was so engulfed in pain. It was all I could do just to take care of my daughter and grieving husband. Now, I realize that it was the in-between times, the days I had spent in the "green pastures" getting to know my Shepherd, that God used to carry me through the valley. All of the truths I had learned about the character of God were now being put into action. Had I not had those things stored in my heart, there would have been nothing to keep my faith intact.

In *My Utmost for His Highest*, Oswald Chambers said, "We imagine we would be alright if a big crisis arose; but the big crisis will only reveal the stuff we are made of, it will not put anything into us." When my heart was filled with fear, the Holy Spirit brought to mind those verses I had fed on regarding peace. The

Word in a very real way became the Shepherd's rod and staff in my life to not only bring comfort, but also protection from the temptation to abandon my faith and belief in the goodness of God.

The Shepherd's comfort visited us in the most unexpected ways. When I discovered I was pregnant with our first baby, I am embarrassed to admit, I was not happy with the timing. We were trying to finish school and I wasn't planning to have a baby yet. However, had we had Natalie after completing school as planned, John's parents would never have been able to see and love her. I would have had a difficult time coping with both death and a new-born.

As it turned out, our daughter was the Shepherd's source of comfort in the shadows. She was His provision for us to get through some very difficult days. From the time Natalie arrived, she filled our home with joy. She became our little Barnabas—"daughter of encouragement." On many occasions her happy, joyful nature lifted our spirits out of the depths of despair, putting smiles on our grief-stricken faces and laughter in our pained hearts. We realized that God has His hidden purposes and plans in the shadows, and we need to trust Him, especially when nothing makes sense.

A week before I sat down to write this chapter, I received yet another phone call: this time it was from my family. I knew something was wrong when I heard my mother's distraught voice over the phone. She broke the heart-wrenching news: my thirty-two-year-old sister, mother of three young children, devoted Christian, has been diagnosed with a rare, incurable cancer. Grappling with the news, I have found myself poring over this psalm for comfort. I don't believe it was a coincidence that the Shepherd had me in this psalm and verse at this desperate moment.

As I have looked to my Shepherd, walking with Him through the shadows once again, I find Him to be all that He promised, not only to me but to my sister and my entire family. "For thou art with me"—He has indeed been with all of us in our deepest sorrow. Looking down the road to the future, my heart is often gripped with fear of what's around the corner—the painful treatments my sister will endure, her kids' and husband's tender emotions, the question marks. That's when I remember that my heart needs to stay turned to the Shepherd, walking with Him and not running ahead, letting Him meet me today.

Wisely, our Shepherd does not open paths for us in advance of our coming. He does not promise us help before help is needed. He does not remove obstacles from our way before we reach them. Yet when we are on the edge of our need (as I am now) our Shepherd's hand is stretched out. The shadows are again descending on my soul, but I am experiencing peace—a deep peace— because I know the Shepherd is with me even in my darkest despair, whether I always feel His presence or not. This is the message of Psalm 23:4.

Parallels from the Eastern Shepherds

The last time we saw the sheep in this psalm, they were in the luxurious pastures and refreshing waters of rest. But now, in verse 4, the path turns downward and winds towards the threatening ravines below. The shepherd is well aware that he is coming to the most dangerous part of the journey with his sheep. He knows that the straightest way home is through a very dark ravine filled with hard, sharp rocks. The cliffs, high on both sides, along with the heavy bushes, make very dark shadows. Wild animals could easily be hidden—animals that could injure or kill the sheep.

What does the shepherd do at this point? He calls his sheep quietly, making the comfortable sounds they are familiar with— remember, they know his voice. They come close to him. He touches each one, speaking their names tenderly. "Just a little further," he whispers. "We'll be out of the shadows soon. I'm right here with you. Don't fear."

The sheep walk softly, huddled confidently behind their shepherd. They follow him, for they know he knows the way through the darkness. They know he will lead them to safety.

What a beautiful picture of what the Lord does for us when we walk through the dark valleys of life! We can picture ourselves as His little lambs, wrapped in His arms, carried by Him, protected by Him, befriended by Him. We must keep His face always before us, making Him the focal point of our thoughts and hearts, until we are convinced that He will lead us safely through!

Matters for the Heart

1. Do you know without a doubt that your Shepherd is always with you, walking "through" every valley with you? If not, what causes you to doubt your Shepherd's presence?

2. How has the Lord met you in the shadows? Think through a recent valley God has walked you through and make a praise list of all the ways He helped and comforted you during that time.

3. What purposes do you think valleys might accomplish in our lives? How has God used your personal valleys to draw you closer to Him? Reflect on this quote as you think about possible purposes for valleys in your life: "Whole, unbruised, unbroken men are of little use to God . . . because they are deficient in agape love" (Unknown).

4. What fears are you facing in your valley? How can you conquer those fears?

5. Memorize Hebrews 13:5–6 as a reminder of the Shepherd's presence in your life. Also meditate on the phrase "Thou art with me."

6. Pray for the sheep you know who are walking through a dark valley. Pray that they will know God's enabling presence. Pray for ways you can comfort them (sending a card, a phone call, a meal; caring for their children; providing ongoing attention; praying with them and for them; giving them time to heal; remembering difficult first anniversaries with a card or a call; validating their feelings; etc.).

Pick one of these ideas and make plans to comfort someone you know who is going through a difficulty.

7. Pray about the valley in your life right now, that you will experience God's very real presence and comfort and grow from it. Reach out to God now and ask to feel His presence, to experience His friendship, and to be supported by His strength.

Matters for Sharing

Chapter 5 reminds us that there is no time in our life when we need the comfort and companionship of our Shepherd more than when we are going through dark and bitter experiences. Consider how you might help someone walk through the shadows in their life while pointing them to the Shepherd.

• Do you know someone who has just lost a loved one? During a difficult time like this it can be comforting to have a friend present. You don't have to say anything, just sit with the person and make yourself available to do anything that needs to be done. You will be showing the person that they are not alone, which will be a great comfort.

• Perhaps you know someone suffering from infertility, illness, depression, or broken dreams. Words have the ability to "minister grace to the hearer" (Ephesians 4:29) and encourage the wounded heart. This can come through the written word, face to face, or by simply making a phone call. Take the time to call someone this week who needs to hear an encouraging word of comfort or support, or send a card.

• Many women who are walking through difficult valleys will experience some form of grief. There are many wonderful books on the market that can help women walk and work through their personal grief. Pray about the right time to give a friend such a book. Assure your friend that grieving is normal with any loss or major change, and help her feel permission to do it. Be available to talk through her grief when she needs to so she can work through the grief stages in a healthy way. Remind her that God is always with her even when she doesn't see or feel Him.

• When pain comes knocking at our door, who cares when the house was last cleaned? It doesn't really matter that the laundry isn't done or the dishes are piling up. Comfort a hurting friend by saying, "I know you've really been going through a tough time lately. Why don't you give me the key to your house and I'll come over tomorrow and clean."

6

Discovering the Shepherd, My Provider and Protector

By Shelly Esser

You prepare a table before me
in the presence of my enemies.
You anoint my head with oil;
my cup overflows.
—Psalm 23:5

How bountifully our Shepherd provides! Looking at verse 5 gives us the great sense that David is completely overwhelmed by the provisions and supply of His Shepherd. He is in such awe that he even changes the setting, to portray a more intimate picture for us of the personal care the Lord has for each of us. The imagery here changes from shepherd and sheep to host and guest. And not just any host either! David introduces us to a most gracious Host who is completely and unreservedly pouring Himself out for us His guests. As a result, our cup overflows!

Lord, give us a new awareness of the overwhelming provisions You graciously give us. Cause our hearts to rise with joy as we grasp just how gracious You have been to us.

Matters for Thought

1. On a scale of one to ten with one being the lowest and ten being the highest, how would you rate your present experience of the abundant life?

2. As you go through the day-to-day demands of life, how aware are you of Christ's constant, overflowing supply for your every need? What makes you aware of this?

Read Psalm 23:5.
3. Although the imagery in verse five has changed from shepherd and sheep to host and guest, what similarities do you notice about the Host's character as compared to the Shepherd's character in the previous four verses? What or who is the focus of this verse?

4. What are the key words in this verse?

a. What message comes through to you personally in these words?

b. What do they teach you about your Shepherd/Host?

5. Why do you think David chose another setting at this point in the psalm? How does this change deepen what he has already portrayed about our Shepherd?

6. What do you think "table" represents in the Christian life?

a. When you think about God "preparing" a table just for you, what does that do for your faith? Your view of God?

b. Have you been sitting recently at the lavish table God especially prepared for you? What keeps you from it?

7. What steps can you take to feed there? It's interesting to note that David used yet another picture of a place to find nourishment from God. Remember the "green pastures?" How does this new picture of nourishment relate to our intimacy with Christ?

8. Verse 4 suggests the "threat" of evil, but in verse five "the presence of my enemies" is reality.

a. What protection does the Lord give us in the face of our enemies according to this verse?

b. How is verse 5 a celebration "in the presence of my enemies"?

9. Verse 5 clearly states that we have enemies. What "enemies" do you encounter in your Christian life?

a. **Read 1 Peter 5:8–9.** What do these verses exhort us to do regarding our greatest enemy, Satan?

b. Why is it important to be alert and watchful?

c. **Read Ephesians 6:10–18.** What spiritual weapons has God provided to believers for spiritual battle?

d. What part do you think prayer has in fighting the battle?

e. **Read 2 Thessalonians 3:3.** Why is it important to keep our focus on our protector, Christ, "in the presence of my enemies?" How do you find comfort in the reality that the battle belongs to the Lord?

" But the Lord is faithful and He will strengthen and protect you from the evil one. "

10. Look up the following verses and write down the uses for oil in Scripture.
Matthew 25:1–13 *be prepared*
Isaiah 1:6; Mark 6:13; Luke 10:34; James 5:14 *healing agents*
1 Samuel 9:15 to 10:1, Leviticus 8:12 *Anointing*
Genesis 28:18 *blessing, gift, offering to God*

related to Holy Spirit often

What uses of oil do you think David had in mind as he wrote Psalm 23?

11. In Scripture, oil is often associated with the Holy Spirit.

a. Why is it important to have a constant and continuing anointing of the Holy Spirit in our lives?

b. What do Acts 1:8, Romans 15:13, Ephesians 3:16, Romans 5:5, and John 15:5 teach us about the Holy Spirit's role in our lives?

12. David talks about experiencing a "full" or "overflowing cup." What might that mean?

13. How does the Host fill your cup to overflowing?

er am I filling it up to overflowing with bad things?

Matters for Reflection

Discovering the Shepherd, My Provider

A man booked passage on a ship that was crossing the Atlantic. He brought with him enough money to buy a ticket, a block of cheese and some crackers for the long voyage. The first few days the crackers and cheese tasted good, but eventually they became stale. Each day as he watched the porters carry large steaks, lobsters, chickens and other delicious foods to the ship's guests, he became very hungry. In fact, he became so hungry that he grabbed one of the porters. "I'll do anything to get one of those steaks," he said. "I'll wash dishes, clean rooms, even mop the deck." The porter replied, "You bought a ticket, didn't you? The meals come with the ticket."

For years I lived the "cheese and cracker" Christian life, resembling the man in the story instead of experiencing the lavish provisions the Lord—my gracious Host—had prepared for me. My Christian life began in junior high, when with the help of my mother, I prayed to ask Jesus into my heart. From that moment on things became dramatically different in my life. I had a deep passion for God and a desire to grow in my relationship with Him.

However, for years, throughout high school, I lived a very frustrated Christian life, not experiencing all I knew God had for me to experience. There was nothing overflowing in my life. When struggles and problems came along, I had no reserve to draw on in order to get through. I was living from "hand to mouth" spiritually, just barely getting by. There were no new insights or spiritual experiences that brought joy. I experienced just salvation and, after that, starvation, in spite of God's great plenty and His willingness to give not just a tiny portion, but an abundant, overflowing one.

Jesus tells us in John 10:10, "I have come that they may have life, and have it to the full." (Some translations say "abundantly.") My life certainly wasn't being lived to the "full." It wasn't even close. I knew God had prepared a lavish table for me, a table of complete supply, a place where I could come and find everything I needed for all of life's challenges and struggles. The trouble was, I didn't know how to appropriate that reality into my life. I didn't know how to come to the table, so I wandered in a "cheese and cracker" spiritual existence for years.

The year after I graduated from high school was spent at Bible school. I knew if I didn't make some changes in my Christian life, I would never become full of all that God wanted for my life. I couldn't continue living my life with an empty cup. Only a few weeks into Bible school, God began to unfold an incredible reality that forever changed my Christian experience. I learned that the moment we become Christians we have the riches of Christ's power through the Holy Spirit who lives in us. In other words, the only way we can experience the abundant or overflowing life that God intends for us is through the power of the Holy Spirit—the person of Christ who lives within us.

"Oil" in Scripture symbolizes the Holy Spirit. In the banquet scene, verse 5 opens with "oil." Oil was used as a gift to the guest from the host. Anointing the guest's head with oil was a sign of joy, of happiness. It was a representation of the sincerest hospitality, above and beyond the requirement of the host. For sheep, oil was used for medicinal purposes. Placed on sheep's noses, it kept flies away. It was also used for binding up the animal's wounds, resulting in an immediate transformation in the sheep's behavior. It was the oil that made the difference. And it is the "oil"—the Holy Spirit—living in you and me, who will make the difference in our lives. What a wonderful Host He is, and what a great thing He does for all who believe and trust Him.

When we become believers, Jesus moves into our lives and He becomes our in-house helper! He brings us all that He is—His righteousness, His right thinking, His right doing, His right acting, His empowerment. It is His incredible power that gives us the ability to live an abundant, exciting Christian life.

Major Ian Thomas of Torchbearers gave a wonderful illustration in a sermon: He says there are some people who are trying to live a life they don't have. They have a car, all right, but no engine, so they go around pushing their car up the hills of their lives trying to make it go and as a result, get worn out and exhausted in the process. They're trying to live a life they don't have. They don't have an engine under the hood. They don't have the power; they're not connected with God. So there is no way they can go beyond the human limitations to do and be what God wants them to be. There is simply no power to do it.

But, he says, there's another group of people. These people are those who have a life they haven't lived. They have an engine in the car and they're still pushing it. What I discovered all those years ago is this: I have always had all I have needed to experience the lavishly abundant life that God desires, but I hadn't been to the source, the Holy Spirit, who would give me the power to live it. Once I realized what was mine in Christ, my cup began to overflow.

We can say, "I'm so tired," and God says, "But I'm not." We say, "I'm so weak, I just don't have the strength to go on," and He answers, "I have the strength for you." We think, "God, I don't have any wisdom for dealing with these kids or this situation at work," He responds, "But I do. I know your kids and what they need. I know about your job." We can tell Him everything we're not, where our own supply is lacking, and God will tell us everything He is and provide us with it, if we let Him. We house His Spirit in us and if we allow that Spirit to operate in our lives, we're going to be OK. He will provide us with everything we need. His supply for us will never run dry!

Verse 5 reveals a gracious Host who desires to prepare a table of provision, resources, and strength not just in the day-to-day challenges of life, but also in the midst of the most distressing circumstances in our lives. We need all He has provided through His Word. We need our power source: the Holy Spirit. To look at the Lord's table of supply is to realize that there is nothing, nothing that is too big for God to handle in our lives. His supply is enough. In 2 Corinthians 12:9, we are reminded, "My grace is sufficient for you, for my power is made perfect in weakness."

Some of you might be thinking, "But you don't understand. You have never been through a divorce . . . a spouse's death . . . a prodigal child . . . the heartache of living day-to-day with an unbelieving spouse . . . with depression." You may be right. But David is trying to tell us that God's supply is enough. When we come to the Lord's table of supply we're going to find just the right helping.

Maybe you need a helping of grace today—He has prepared it. Or maybe it's a helping of protection, forgiveness, boldness to witness, patience, strength, hope, joy, or rest from weariness. Perhaps you're in the valley and you need a portion of endurance, a bowl of strength, and a platter of forgiveness. Whatever your need is, David is encouraging us to "come to the table," for our gracious Host has everything we need! His supply is always in the present. He doesn't give us helpings for tomorrow, but for today. If we come and sit at His table, we will always be satisfied, never going away hungry. Our cup will run over with His unending supply!

Discovering a Cup Overflowing

Cup in Scripture is used figuratively for blessings and is often associated with joy, which is the case in this verse. *Cup* can also mean life's experiences—good, bad, and indifferent—to which we're exposed. The idea of a "full cup" here is one that is overflowing, abundant, exceeding in measure—above the ordinary. It speaks of the spiritual benefits that are ours as His own. The cup we have, as Christians, is completely overflowing only when we let the Lord fill it. Unfortunately, so often we walk around half-filled because we're content to let other things fill our cups. Things like people, ambitions, busyness, self-efforts, or church activities. In the end, they will always leave us empty because we were created to find our satisfaction, our joy, our fullness in God alone.

If we're at the table of the Lord Jesus Christ, our cups will never go empty or be inadequately filled. As Roy Lessin points out, "He is not the God of the 'half empty' or 'half full' in our lives, He is the God of the exceedingly abundantly above all we could ask or think. When He fills our cup, it is overflowing." For every need there will be ample supply, a supply so abundant that it will overflow out of our lives and into the lives of those around us.

Carol Mayhall in her book, *Filled to Overflowing*, writes this:

The character of God—who He is—will completely satisfy us if we open ourselves fully to Him. That doesn't mean He doesn't want us to have the "pluses" in life. He wants to delight us with bonuses of every scope and variety. But bonuses . . . pluses . . . extras are just additional things. They are not the things that are necessary in order for joy, peace, hope, understanding, and all the other ingredients with which we are to be filled.

If we are filled full with God Himself, then even joy, peace and hope are by-products. They are the result of God in us.

So may our focus be on Him. May our dwelling be in Him. May our strength be through Him. May our joy, peace, hope and understanding be by Him. Until at last, we are filled to overflowing with God Himself.

‎ Heart

1. Have you been living "hand to mouth" spiritually, failing to embrace the abundant provisions the Lord has prepared for you? What steps can you take today to begin living the abundant life?

2. What is your life in need of today—where do you need His supply? Where have you been turning for your supply in the last month or week—your spouse, your family, your bank account? Only at the table of God's supply will you discover help for your deepest need. Tell God today that you will come to the table and dine with Him, letting His supply completely fill you.

3. In what areas of your life have you been trying to live the Christian life on your own power, your own strength, apart from the Holy Spirit? Ask the Holy Spirit to fill you now and begin yielding your life to Him.

4. Meditate on this quote: "You can't and God never said you could. He can and He always said He would." Have you been treating God as if He were of minor importance?

5. Read Ephesians 5:18. Have you been filled with the Spirit and experienced the Spirit's guidance in your life? (The more you get to know what's yours as a believer, the sooner you'll experience the abundant life.)

6. Is your cup running over today? Are you experiencing the power of the Holy Spirit in your day-to-day life with your spouse, in your mothering, on the job? Where you hurt? Where you struggle? Is your cup running over today in your experience with your Host/Shepherd? If not, in what areas of your life do you need to experience more of Jesus? Meditate on verse 5—for it tells us that we can have a "full cup" as our daily experience.

7. Do the world and those around you look at your life and see a life that is overflowing with Christ and all of His abundant provisions? If not, what changes can you make to become a better witness to those around you? Take steps to make changes and pray for the Lord's help.

Matters for Sharing

This chapter brings our focus to the reality that God's supply is abundant enough. He will give us exactly what we need at the right time to help us through whatever we're facing. Think about how you might show others that God will meet all of their needs. Find some creative ways to give away some of what the Lord has abundantly given you.

• Every community has service-oriented outreaches to provide for the needy. Do some research and find out about your community's soup kitchens, food pantries, homeless shelters, or shelters for abused women and children (you can look these up in the yellow pages or check with the local churches). Set up a time when you can go help with one of these types of programs, modeling the message that God loves and provides.

• Is there a needy family in your area who you could help both practically and materially? If you don't know of one, ask one of the area churches for a name. Then be Christ's provision for this family. Gather clothes for their kids, or like-new toys that are just in need of a good home. By doing the practical, you will be Christ's provision for these people as you provide for them in ways they couldn't themselves.

• Do you have a friend or family member who has tried everything to fill the empty place in her life? Take her to a Bible study, mom's group, or to hear a speaker on how God is the only one who can fill the needs in her life. Afterward, talk to her about what she heard, and ask if she would like to attend again.

• Sometimes the smallest gestures can have the greatest impact. Consider these ideas for reaching out to those you encounter who need to know that they have a Shepherd who wants to provide for them.

A timely magazine article. Give someone an article about God's provision for her during a difficult time. Be on the alert for testimonies that can be shared with your non-Christian friends.

Booklets. Pocket-sized booklets with inspiring poetry, Scripture verses on specific topics, and messages about trusting God abound. One might be just right for your co-worker or neighbor who's upset about an illness, job loss, or troubled marriage.

Small laminated cards or plaques. Look for messages of encouragement such as "God is in control." Think of friends you can give these cards to; someone who's anxious, lonely, stressed, or depressed.

Weekly phone calls. We underestimate the impact of a phone call saying we care. Think of someone who needs encouragement or is lonely. Plan a time on a weekly basis when you can call her. It doesn't have to be a long conversation. Just the thoughtfulness of remembering a hurting person will go a long way in conveying God's shepherd love.

7

Discovering My Faithful Shepherd

By Marcia Bueschel

*Surely goodness and love will follow me
all the days of my life,
and I will dwell in the house of the Lord
forever.*

—Psalm 23:6

As we approach the final verse of this beautiful psalm, notice the confidence with which David speaks. He doesn't say "perhaps" or "maybe," he says "surely!" After spending several weeks studying Psalm 23, we hope that you are able to echo David's words as he comes to important conclusions about his life with the Shepherd.

Lord, as we close our study on Psalm 23, we thank You for your faithfulness to us. Help us to place our confidence in Your faithfulness, just as David did.

Matters for Thought

1. How would you define confidence?

2. Considering your daily life, list in who or what you have confidence.

Read through the entire psalm, then reread verse 6.
3. Looking over the entire psalm, of what is David certain?

4. Scripture is filled with many assurances—promises that we can rely on as believers. Spend some time looking up and discussing the following verses and write the theme for each grouping.

- Deuteronomy 7:9
  Psalm 89:1
  Psalm 119:90
  Philippians 1:6

• Psalm 103:12
  Matthew 11:28–30
  John 1:12–13
  2 Timothy 1:9
  Titus 3:5

• John 3:16, 36
  John 5:24
  John 10:28
  1 John 5:10–13

5. What can the Lord's promises do for us?

6. *Zondervan's Pictorial Dictionary* defines mercy as "1. Forbearance from inflicting punishment upon a . . . lawbreaker or 2. that compassion which causes one to help the weak, the sick or the poor."

a. How did the Lord show mercy to David?

b. How does He show mercy to us?

c. How do both of the above definitions apply to us?

7. Phillip Keller says, "Just as God's goodness and mercy flow to me all the days of my life, so goodness and mercy should follow me, should be left behind me, as a legacy to others." As we have previously discussed, we are not only sheep but also shepherds. Mercy is listed as one of the fruits of the Spirit in Galatians 5:22–23. How can we show goodness and mercy to those around us?

8. The Lord can, and does, bring goodness out of our bleak circumstances. Think of a time in your life when the Lord brought good from a difficult situation. Share it with the others.

9. In some situations, the goodness that comes may not arrive for years. In the meantime, what can we do?

10. When has the Lord has been faithful to you in ways that surprised you?

11. Over the past few weeks, we have looked at some of David's emotional highs and lows.
a. How can he make the statement that goodness and mercy have followed him all the days of his life? Do you believe him?

b. What must you do to reach that point of agreeing with David's words?

12. David speaks of dwelling "in the house of the Lord forever." Read John 14:1–7. These words were spoken during Jesus' final time alone with His chosen disciples. He had just finished washing their feet, and Judas had left the room. Because Jesus knew what was ahead of Him, we believe that He wanted not only to teach, but also to comfort His friends.

a. Whose house is Jesus talking about? What is significant about a house?

b. Thomas asked a good question in verse 5. (Aren't you glad he asked it?) What reassurance does Jesus give?

c. How do we know that this promise applies to us?

Matters for Reflection

Our Attitudes

David ends this psalm filled with happy enthusiasm. Some of us are born pessimists—it's hard for us to see any good, ever! Do you know someone like that? Or perhaps you can identify? If you tend to be pessimistic, it may help to spend time with someone who is more optimistic. You might gain a more balanced perspective.

I have found this to be true in my marriage. Dave and I are often thinking and feeling just the opposite of each other. By spending time together, we usually reach a more balanced view. I once heard that an optimist is someone who believes that things can't possibly get any better than they are right now, and a pessimist fears that this is true! How we view our current situation seems to depend very much on our attitudes. David has given us a glimpse into his life and his attitudes in this psalm—he has revealed his solemnity, as well as his bubbly confidence in his Shepherd.

Our Circumstances

Along with our attitudes, we must consider our circumstances. When we spend time with friends and loved ones who may be going through difficult times, we need to be careful how we encourage them. I believe that one of the best things we can do for someone is to listen well. Have you ever found yourself pouring out your heart to a trusted friend, only to have her make light of your situation, brushing you away with a, "I know just what you're going through, and, believe me, you'll be just fine"? When you find yourself listening to someone's heartfelt sadness, it is not helpful to make light of the situation, or remind her or him that all will be well in the end. You do not know what that person may have to endure, and I believe that we have no right to minimize another person's pain.

You also don't need to try and cheer her up. Ecclesiastes 3:3–4 reminds us that there is a time for weeping and a time for laughter, a time for mourning and a time to dance. Romans 12:15 says to "Rejoice with those who rejoice; mourn with those who mourn."

To help those who are hurting you can provide a listening ear, let them know you genuinely care, and remind them that the Lord cares, too. Perhaps this is one of the ways that we can have goodness and mercy follow after us.

Our Future

David ends his psalm looking forward to that day when he will dwell in the house of the Lord forever. He somehow has a glimpse of being a part of his Shepherd's flock for eternity, though the first five books of the Bible—the only Bible David had—don't clearly describe heaven. David didn't lose the hope or optimism of his youth. He found his Shepherd to be reliable and changeless, and he looked forward to spending eternity in the flock. Keller speaks of "A sheep so deeply satisfied with the flock to which it belongs, with the ownership of this particular shepherd that it has no wish to change whatsoever."

Notice that David's faith is focused on his Shepherd, not on the green pastures or the still waters that his Shepherd provides. He ends his psalm with the final assurance that no matter what life brings him, no matter what valleys he must go through or what evils he must face, he will be spending "forever" in the house of the Lord. We don't know what heaven will be like, although there are many references to it in the New Testament; but we do know that we will be with the Lord. Someone once said that what makes a house inviting is the person who lives there. As believers, we can view heaven as inviting because we know the One who lives there.

"Heaven is a prepared place for a prepared people."
—Unknown

Matters for the Heart

1. Look over the entire psalm and determine which verse you can identify most with right now. Why?

2. David speaks of the Lord's faithfulness to him in the past, as well as into the future. In your current circumstances, what is one area in which you can begin to start trusting the Lord?

3. Spend time in prayer for those around you who are in difficult circumstances. Is there some way you can be of encouragement?

4. Choose one of the verses discussed today that is especially meaningful to you and commit it to memory.

Matters for Sharing

With assurance, we can rest in the Shepherd's goodness and mercy. He has our best and eternal interests in His mind. Throughout this psalm you have found hope and encouragement. Now is the time to share that hope with others.

• Consider starting a Bible study in your home. There are numerous studies that can be worked through together one-on-one or as a small group.

• On the National Day of Prayer, post an invitation to meet before work begins so you can spend time praying together.

• Use the *Steps to Leading a Person to Christ* in the back of this study guide to help someone know the Lord. Remember that you can be one of the Lord's shepherds to those around you—your children, your spouse, your family and your friends.

Leader's Guide

My Cup Overflows

A Deeper Study of Psalm 23

Introduction to Leader's Guide

Purpose

This section is meant to guide the facilitator through leading a small group of no more than ten people. As a leader, you may or may not feel comfortable in a teaching capacity, but you may have had some group experience. These notes will give you some insight into the more difficult questions and provide you with some additional ideas. You should be able to lead the discussion using the information provided, but you may also wish to do further research. We have tried to give you a general sense of our thoughts as we were preparing this study guide. A *Matters for Sharing* section is included at the end of each chapter for the purpose of applying the material and providing an outreach that can either be done individually or as a group.

Suggestions

• Each leader's guide includes an **If Time Is Short** section. This section will list questions from the study that we feel are most important. If time is running short, these are the questions to concentrate on.

• The format we planned for this study was:

1. **Welcome time:** Fifteen minutes of socializing with beverages and something light to eat—pastry or fresh fruit, for example.

2. **Small group time:** No more than 1 1/2 hours. If there are more than ten people, you may wish to divide into two small groups. In larger groups, discussion may be stifled.

• We have divided the study guide as follows:

-First fifteen minutes for "getting-to-know-you" or icebreaker questions

-Forty-five minutes for the main body of the lesson

-Final fifteen minutes for prayer and application time and outreach suggestions

This brings the total study to less than two hours, which, in our experience, is desired by those who have attended.

We suggest that the study guides be made available before the first meeting, and that participants come to each meeting with the lesson completed or at least overviewed. However, the facilitator needs to be aware that not everyone will be able to do this. We have found that even if only a few participants come prepared, the entire discussion flows better, and those who aren't prepared seem to participate more.

Chapter One Leader's Guide

Objective

To give an overview and lay the foundation for the study of the psalm, and to discover that in every situation, we can experience Christ as the Shepherd of our lives.

Personal Preparation

• Read Psalms 22, 23, and 24 to get familiar with the context of the Shepherd psalms.
• Read through Psalm 23 several times in several different translations.
• Spend ten to fifteen minutes meditating and reflecting on the psalm.
• Focus on God as your Shepherd and what that means in your life personally.
• Pray for each woman in your group, even though you may not have met together.
• Select three or four questions from the Matters for the Heart section to include in your discussion.

Leading the Group

Before launching into the questions, open the group with prayer. When you pray, remember the main purpose of your study. Ask and expect the Holy Spirit to teach the group, especially you, the leader. Allow the freedom for a few others to pray briefly, at the beginning, if they like. Then read the passage from a familiar translation, so that everyone has an opportunity to think about the text before diving into the questions.

Questions 1–3: Use these first questions as ice-breakers. Be willing to offer your own answers first to get the group started and then wait for others to share. Ask the group to share their favorite verse in the psalm and why they selected that particular one.

Questions 7–9: Together the three Shepherd psalms portray a complete picture of Christ. Psalm 22 tells of Christ's death on the Cross as Savior, giving His life for the sheep. This psalm speaks of the joy of salvation, what it means to have been put into a right relationship with Jesus Christ. Psalm 23 presents Christ as the Great Shepherd, giving His love and provisions to His sheep. This psalm is descriptive of what it feels like to be at home with God, enjoying a personal relationship with Him.

Psalm 24 completes the picture by portraying Christ as the Chief Shepherd. This psalm speaks of expectation, telling us what it will be like when He appears again to claim His own. You will need to explain that only as one has acquired a personal relationship with the Good Shepherd in Palm 22 can she know Him as the Great Shepherd of Psalm 23. We must know the Shepherd in Psalm 22 before we can come to Psalm 23 and say the "Lord is my Shepherd." This psalm only brings true comfort as one has acquired a personal relationship with Him (See the *Steps to Leading a Person to Christ* at the end of this book).

Psalm 23 clearly teaches that the Lord is not everyone's Shepherd. There has to come a moment in our lives when we say "yes" to Christ. Unless we come to terms with our own failure, rebellion and sin (the sheep syndrome), we will never go on to experience all God has for us as demonstrated in Psalm 23.

Question 10a: Scholars agree that David wrote Psalm 23. It is believed that the psalm was written later in David's life, very likely towards the end of it. However, David the king never forgot David the shepherd boy; so he used this beautiful picture of the shepherd caring for his sheep to compare with our relationship with God.

Question 10b: It is believed that David was viewing the Shepherd throughout the psalm, but in two different roles. In verses 1–4, he sees the Shepherd in direct relationship to His care for the sheep, and in verses 5–6 he sees the Shepherd as a gracious Host at His large tent where He cares for His guests during a banquet.

Question 11: This is a very important observation in understanding the psalm. Every verb, you will notice, is in the present tense, representing God's ministry in our lives today, at this moment. This clearly points to the personal nature and involvement of God in our lives.

Questions 12–13: The Shepherd is the key to the entire psalm. This is the most important element in this study. Much, if not most, of the truths set forth in the psalm will be missed unless you take the Shepherd you meet in verse one through the entire psalm. We need to be careful here that we don't divorce the "things" in the psalm from the Shepherd. Otherwise, the psalm will become just a repetition of things the Shepherd provides.

Question 15: These are some common characteristics of sheep: require the most care and supervision of all domestic animals, compelled to mob instinct, fearful, timid, dumb, destructive, stubborn, wanderers, vulnerable to predators, and dirty. When an adequate relationship exists between a sheep who freely admits he needs a shepherd and the shepherd who cares and leads in wisdom and love, the sheep begin to demonstrate great qualities not previously apparent.

Close your group study in a time of prayer. Use the prayer exercise at the end of the Matters for the Heart section. Spend about ten minutes and then close.

If Time Is Short
For an abbreviated lesson, concentrate on these questions in Chapter One: 1, 3, 5, 6, 7, 9, 10, 11, 13, and 14.

Chapter Two Leader's Guide

Objective

To understand that our Heavenly Father loves and cares for us as a shepherd cares for his sheep, and through His example, to better shepherd those around us.

Personal Preparation

• Again, read through Psalms 22, 23, and 24 to reacquaint yourself with the context of the Shepherd psalms.

• Pray for the women in your group.

• Become familiar with the Steps to Leading a Person to Christ, found at the back of this book, so that you can help those with questions.

• Plan to spend the final fifteen minutes covering Matters for the Heart. Spend some silent time on the first suggestion, so that group members can make their lists of blessings. This chapter then devotes time for prayer. Some of these points help apply the scriptures to our lives, as well. Be sensitive to your particular group. Some people may feel more comfortable dwelling on these points in silence, especially since group members may still be getting to know one another.

Leading the Group

Questions 1–3: These are openers. Spend no more than fifteen minutes on them.

Question 4: For those who are interested, the following will give you a detailed study of the descriptive names David used. Try to place each name of God into the proper verse of Psalm 23.

• Genesis 22:13–14, Jehovah-jireh "The LORD will provide"
• Exodus 15:26, Jehovah-rapha "The LORD that heals"
• Judges 6:24, Jehovah-shalom "The LORD, our peace"
• Jeremiah 23:6, Jehovah-tsidkenu "The LORD our righteousness"
• Ezekiel 48:35, Jehovah-shammah "The LORD ever present"
• Exodus 17:8–15, Jehovah-nissi "The LORD our banner"
• Psalm 23:1, Jehovah-raah "The LORD my shepherd" (Baxter, Vol. 3,125)

David used the names he knew for God and made a poem. A similar exercise for us would be to take the descriptive names of the Holy Spirit—like Guide, Counselor, Comforter, Teacher—and make a poem of them.

Question 5: If your Bible does not provide this information, check a Bible dictionary. The point is that David uses the most exalted, holy name for God, and yet he also calls Him his Shepherd. God is not only majestic, He is also personal.

Question 6: Some people see God as a Santa Claus, ready to give them anything they want. Others may see Him as an ogre ready to punish them over the smallest offense. By the end of this book, we hope that your group members will have a realistic, balanced perspective. Consider that much of how we view our Heavenly Father comes from our attitudes towards our earthly fathers.

Question 13b: We are meant to have a full life in Christ. You might want to ask what "full life" means. Another question you could ask is, "How does Satan steal the fullness from your life?"

Question 14b: Though Peter and Paul spoke specifically to the elders of the church, we believe this verse can be applied to all of us as Christians. The group needs to think about their relationships and become aware that they may be in shepherding positions, perhaps as parents, teachers, or co-workers.

Question 19: If you live in an affluent society, wants can easily seem like needs. An additional question could be, "How can we keep a check on all the wants in our lives?"

If Time Is Short

For an abbreviated lesson, concentrate on these questions in Chapter Two: 4, 6, 7, 8, 9, 10, 11, 13a, 14a and 14b, 17, 18, 19, and 20.

Chapter Three Leader's Guide

Objective

To recognize how the Shepherd provides places of spiritual nourishment and refreshment for us, through the "green pastures" of His Word, and to learn to follow His leading by feeding regularly

Personal Preparation

• If you have not been feeding regularly on God's Word, spend this coming week getting back on track.

• Bring some devotional resources that have been helpful to you and share them with the group.

• Read Psalm 119 and make a list of all the ways the Word provides nourishment, refreshment, leading, and peace for us. Be prepared to share some of your discoveries as you go through the study, particularly as you discuss question 10.

• Think about how God has specifically used the Word in your own life. Be prepared to share some of those examples with the group to encourage them to get into the Word.

• Pray for the women in your group every day this week.

• Plan to go over questions 2, 3, and 6 in the Matters for the Heart section and pray for one another in areas of need.

Leading the Group

Open with prayer. Read Psalm 23:1–2 emphasizing the second verse, this week's study. Begin by sharing something the Lord has done to nourish and refresh your soul this past week.

Questions 1–3: Use these three questions as lead-in questions to the study. Perhaps begin with Corrie ten Boom's quote for discussion. The intent is for the women to be examining their own lives, so that they can begin recognizing what areas in their lives need spiritual nourishment and refreshment.

Questions 4–6: These questions lead you into the verse itself. Help the group begin to draw our their own observations from the text, interpreting what they think it means. This verse clearly points out to us the benefits and blessings that are ours because we belong to the Shepherd. It is important to emphasize the *who*—the Shepherd. For it is the Shepherd that makes possible all spiritual nourishment, refreshment, rest, and peace.

Questions 7–8: Help the group understand the role of peace in experiencing rest. What is true for sheep is true for us; rest is impossible without peace. Read and discuss Romans 5:1 and Philippians 4:7 together. Make sure the group understands the difference between "peace with God" and the "peace of God." (You will want to be particularly sensitive here as any unbelievers in the group will lack the understanding of needing the experience of "peace with God"—see *Steps to Leading a Person to Christ*, at the end of the book, for help.) The peace spoken of in Romans 5:1 is the peace every believer has with God. The sinner has surrendered and has accepted the peace terms of Calvary. Through faith he now has peace about his sin and his guilt. He now has "peace with God." However, Philippians 4:7 speaks of an entirely different kind of peace. The peace of Romans 5:1 comes with salvation; the peace of Philippians 4:7 keeps us free from worry, fear, and unbelief, for it stems from the daily loving care of our Heavenly Shepherd who is too good to be unkind and too wise to make mistakes with our lives. This is the application of verse two.

Question 10: Read several of these verses aloud and discuss the different ways the Shepherd uses the Word of God in your life. At this time, you could share your findings from Psalm 119. Close your group study in a time of prayer. Keep each other accountable this coming week in your time spent in the Word.

If Time Is Short
For an abbreviated lesson, concentrate on these questions in Chapter Three: 2, 3, 4a, 5, 6, 7, 8, 10, and 11.

Chapter Four Leader's Guide

Objective
To understand that our Heavenly Father is always present and willing to restore our souls and be our guide, if we will ask Him to.

Personal Preparation
- Read 2 Samuel 11:1 to 12:13. This will give you the background story of David's affair with Bathsheba.
- Read Psalm 51. This is David's prayer to his Holy God, a plea for restoration. Psalm 42:5 is a good example of the distress David sometimes felt.
- Pray for the women in your group and ask for guidance. Be aware that the Lord can deal with all our mistakes and sins, big and small, whether it is an adulterous relationship or a cruel word spoken in reproach.
- Once you have worked through this study, spend time thinking about how the Lord has restored your own soul. Share your examples with others in your group, to encourage them.
- Be certain to allow fifteen minutes at the end of the session to cover Matters for the Heart.

Leading the Group
Verse 3 is clearly divided into two sections. In David's case, we frequently see a strong connection between his despair and his sinful lifestyle. This is not always the case, however. Please make it clear to your group members that our souls can be restored daily, just by dwelling upon the Lord's goodness and love for us. We do not need to have made a big mistake to feel His loving presence and healing touch.

Questions 1–5 are opening questions. Spend no more than fifteen minutes on them.

Question 1: This is meant to be a lead-in question. There are many descriptions for our different emotions, but they usually will fall into one of the following: mad, sad, glad, afraid, hurt, and ashamed.

Question 7: Please notice that David uses the present verb tense, indicating that restoring one's soul takes place more than once. David is referring to something other than our initial restoration through salvation. He is speaking of a sheep that is already part of the flock. This is an important point, because our Lord is there to restore us, not just once, but on a continuing basis. A review of David's life would show that he could have felt the need for restoration many times. For example, he had many problems with Saul who was jealous of him, he knew his affair with Bathsheba was wrong, and his firstborn child died shortly after birth.

The following additional information may be helpful in understanding our souls:
- The mind is our contemplative and rational self.
- Our hearts reflect our attitudes.
- For better or worse, our wills help us to choose and decide.
- Our spirits are ourselves apart from earthly connections.

Question 9: The answer might include dealing with the hard issues of life—illnesses, death of someone you love, a willful child who is constantly "butting heads" with you, or financial problems. It may also include wandering away from your loving Shepherd, going off on your own, perhaps even doing things you know to be contrary to His divine will. It can include feeling burdened by the cares of this world or society's ills. The list is endless.

Question 11: Stuart Briscoe has a good suggestion regarding following the correct paths. He advises that we first need to maintain a right attitude of following Jesus as Shepherd. Then we can use our wills, insights, and decision-making abilities, check our options, evaluate, get advice from those we respect, explore the consequences, then go ahead—trusting that the Shepherd will stop you if you're wrong.

Before prayertime, it might be helpful for you to share an area of your life where you need restoring, or have been restored, and an area where you need guidance. This may help others feel more comfortable. These do not need to be "soul-baring" requests. For example, as a wife, mom, and professional, I need the Lord's constant guidance to keep a balance in my life.

If Time Is Short

For an abbreviated lesson, concentrate on these questions in Chapter Four: 1, 6, 7, 8, 9, 10, and 12.

Chapter Five Leader's Guide

Objective

To discover that the Shepherd is our constant companion, especially as we walk through the dark experiences of life (that aloneness and isolation are impossible for the Christian, because God is always with us), and that He not only promises us His presence, but His comfort as well.

Personal Preparation

• Read Psalm 23:4 in several different translations, taking special note of the language changes from the *Lord* and *He* in verses 1–3 to *You* in verses 4–5, referring to God.

• Become familiar with Isaiah 43:1–3, Hebrews 13:5–6, and 2 Corinthians 1:3–4 before the group meets to be able to facilitate the best discussion.

• Think about your own valley experiences. Select one such experience to share with the group, encouraging them with how you experienced God's presence and comfort in your life at the time.

• Find an inspirational story or illustration of someone who has exhibited trust while walking with their Shepherd through their valley. Read it to the group for encouragement. (Example: Joni Eareckson Tada) You may want to open the study with this.

• Pray for special sensitivity this week as you come to the group. There may be several women going through particularly difficult valleys. Think of ways you can encourage them throughout the week, and ways the group can minister to them. Perhaps they may need a card or a meal—be creative and sensitive, asking God for direction and ideas.

• Select several questions from the Matters for the Heart section to discuss before you conclude your time in praying for one another. Be prepared to spend extended time in prayer and less time in discussion should you have group members hurting right now.

• Begin with prayer, asking God to make the truths of this verse reality for the women in your group, especially any going "through the valley" now. Read Psalm 23:1–4, rereading verse 4 in several different translations.

Leading the Group

Questions 1–2: Use these questions to get the discussion time going in a non-threatening atmosphere. You may want to start the discussion off with your own valley experience.

Questions 3–4: Let the women draw their own conclusions here first. This will help them not only make their own discoveries about God's Word, but also help them learn some inductive study principles as well. After they have gleaned all they can, you can share some of your own observations.

Questions 5–6: "Even though" implies that we will go through valleys. This is consistent with Scripture, for in James 1:2 and John 16:33 we are told that this is so. The important point to bring out is that "acceptance" has a lot to do with getting through the valleys. As we accept the fact that we will go through difficult things, we'll be able to better relax in God's promises of both His presence and His empowerment.

Question 7: "Shadow of death" in the Hebrew is not necessarily an explicit reference to death, but it does refer to all dark and bitter experiences, one of which may be death. So in the common usage of the passage, the thought of death need not be excluded. The imagery used here is consistent with the Shepherd metaphor used in the psalm because the shepherd leads his flock through ravines where the steep and narrow slopes keep out the light. The idea of the "shadow of death" can also refer to a passage or transition in life, as well as the bitter and dark experiences of life (valley of loneliness, persecution, unemployment, broken relationships, disappointments, exhaustion, lost friendships, moving, rejection, grief, spiritual dryness and distance).

Question 8: The key to this verse is found in the phrase "for you are with me." Here, David doesn't argue that it is so. He confidently tells that it is true! At this point, you may want to ask your group if they believe that. We have the promises from God's Word that when sorrow and affliction come our way, as they will, the Shepherd will go with us through every one of them and will see to it that we are not overcome by them. You may want to emphasize here, however, that we have something to do. It is our responsibility to keep our eye on the Shepherd, and trust Him through the valleys. Ask your group to reflect on this quote by George Mueller, "My eye is not on the density of the fog [or valley] but on the living God, who controls every circumstance in my life." It is in the hour of our deepest sorrow that we discover how sustaining our Shepherd really is.

Question 9: As we dissect this verse, this little word could easily be overlooked, yet it holds some of the greatest comfort when confronting the valleys of life. Share your dictionary definition of the word *through* with the group. This little word rings with hope, implying that there is a way out, that the valleys (at least some of them) in our lives are not forever. There is light somewhere beyond the shadows. The comfort comes as we realize that we do not remain in the valley, the darkness, but we pass through it. You may want to point out that there will be some lasting valleys in life we won't walk through this side of heaven (a chronic illness or health condition, for example), but the Shepherd still provides light in the shadows and His enduring presence.

Question 10: One of the greatest enemies of sheep is fear. When afraid, sheep often panic and scatter, causing injury or death. This is probably one of our greatest enemies, as well, in the valley (fear of the unknown, of pain, of what can happen, of how to cope). You will want to focus on faith here, because it is our faith in a living, personal God that will save us from uncontrollable panic in the face of danger. We do not need to fear evil because God is greater than evil and He will protect us. The sentiment here is that the

Lord is our Shepherd so we don't need to fear because He is always with us. It is His presence that encourages us to go through the fear.

Questions 13–16: There is probably no greater need for comfort in our lives than when walking through the valley. The rod and staff were the shepherd's instruments of comfort for their sheep as their function was to protect, guide, prod, and even to discipline the sheep. You will want to discuss the need for bringing practical comfort to those who are suffering around you, how you can be their rod and staff. One of the primary purposes for the difficulties we go through is to be able to practice a comfort ministry with those whom God has placed us. Discuss the quote, "Whole, unbruised, unbroken men are of little use to God . . . because they are deficient in agape love."

If Time Is Short

For an abbreviated lesson, concentrate on these questions in Chapter Five: 2, 3, 4, 5, 7, 9, 11, 12, and 13.

Chapter Six Leader's Guide

Objective

To begin to grasp all the abundant provisions the Lord has prepared for us in our day-to-day experience, and discover the role of the Holy Spirit in our lives.

Personal Preparation

• Read Psalm 23:5 several times, observing the scene changes in this verse. Think through why David might have changed the metaphor at this point in the psalm.

• Do some additional study this week on the role of the Holy Spirit in the believer's life. You will want to have a good grasp of this to be able to clearly communicate it and the importance to your group. (See Romans 6:11, Galatians 2:20, Ephesians 5:18, Acts 1:8, Romans 15:13, Ephesians 3:16, Romans 5:5, John 15:5, Galatians 5:22–23.)

• Look back over your Christian experience, and write down some of the ways you have seen God supply you with your every need. Plan to share some of these personal examples with your group.

• Pray for each woman in your group every day this week. Pray specifically that she will come into an understanding of the abundant Christian life and the role of the Holy Spirit in helping her live it.

• Be sure to end your group time with application and prayer. Go over questions 1-6 in the Matters for the Heart section. Have each woman share one action step for the week.

Open with prayer and dig right into the verse, Psalm 23:5, by reading it aloud. You may want to share a personal illustration of God's supply in your own life, or discuss the following statistic about how few Christians are indeed experiencing the daily overflowing life that is available to them: Dr. Billy Graham has stated that at least ninety percent of all Christians in America are living defeated lives. Ask the group why they think this is the case.

Leading the Group

Questions 1–2: These ice-breaker questions will lead naturally from your introduction above.

Questions 3–5: The women who have done their homework will be able to offer the group some of their own observations and interpretations at this point. Allow time for women to share their discoveries of God's Word, and then share your own. Most writers associate this scene with a wealthy host and his lavish provision for an oriental banquet. In fact, it is likely some type of "thanksgiving" banquet. The thanksgiving idea is very significant because the psalmist has recently passed through difficult circumstances and danger. The emphasis is on God's present supply for our every need.

Question 6: We need to know something about Eastern hospitality to understand this verse. In the East, a feast was a special occasion where very special preparations took place, much like our Thanksgiving dinner. The host made sure that everything was done perfectly. The guests were given only the best. When David said, "you prepare a table before me," he was saying "you supply me with my every need." The table symbolized God's supply and represents the place where we can come and meet with Him. His supply for our lives is always adequate and we will always leave His table full. Spend some time discussing questions 6a and 6b to bring out this application.

Question 8: David was comforted that the Lord provided for him in the presence of his enemies. Despite impending danger, the Lord spread out a table for him. Much of David's life was characterized by fear, flight, and reliance on others for hospitality. Many times as a young man and king he found himself dining with his enemies surrounding him, in the protection of his host. The Lord was his protector, and He is ours.

Question 9: 1 Peter 5:8–9 clearly tells us our greatest enemy is Satan. Enemies in the Christian life can take on many other faces:

impatience, pride, selfishness, materialism, our sinful natures, worldliness, people. The temptations we face can also become our enemies if we're not careful. "Enemies" can be seen as those things that keep our focus off God, and Satan uses all kinds of things to do that. We need to remember when facing enemies of the Christian life that God will protect us from the evil one (2 Thessalonians 3:3, 1 John 4:4). As we daily place ourselves under God's care and protection, we will receive the victory needed for the war that has already been won. The battle belongs to the Lord!

Questions 10–11: Christians not only need to know what is available to us in the Christian life, we also need to know how to experience God's lavish supply on a daily basis. Perhaps at this point in the study women are saying, "Yes, I want this kind of experience and relationship with my Shepherd/Host, but how do I get it?" In Scripture, oil symbolizes the Holy Spirit. The Holy Spirit living in us makes the difference. We can try to be the shepherds of our own lives, to control everything, to decide what pasture to go to, and end up completely frustrated. We have to remind ourselves that all God ever asks us to be is sheep or guests and He is the Shepherd and Host of our lives. We need to yield our lives to Christ, letting Him live through us. Thoroughly go over the verses listed in question 11b and discuss the importance of the Holy Spirit in the Christian life.

Close the group in prayer, particularly praying through the applications in the Matters for the Heart section. Pray that each woman would begin to discover the role of the Holy Spirit in her life.

If Time Is Short
For an abbreviated lesson, concentrate on these questions in Chapter Six: 1, 2, 4b, 5, 6a, 7, 8, 9e, 10, 11, and 12.

Chapter Seven Leader's Guide

Objective

To understand that we are always in the care of the Lord, and that He will bring about goodness from our circumstances and show us mercy, both now and forever, because we are His children.

Personal Preparation

Once again, read through the entire Psalm 23 to review the overall message.

• Read John 14:1–7, one of Jesus' pictures of heaven. Become familiar with the context. Who is Jesus talking to? When does this take place?

• If this is the end of your sessions together, or you want to take a short break before starting another study, we recommend that you have an idea for a special activity next week such as sharing a meal together. If you suggest the idea, your group can then plan it together. This is a good way to nourish blossoming friendships and encourage involvement.

Leading the Group

Questions 1–4: As an opener, lead the group to discuss what confidence is, how it is manifested in society, and what our confidence is dependent upon. To illustrate this concept, I appreciate Stuart Briscoe's sermon illustration of faith and walking on thin ice. If ice is thick, even though you may have only a small amount of faith in it, that ice will support you. If ice is thin, however, you can have a tremendous amount of faith in it, but it's not going to hold you up. I think this can also apply to confidence. It is not how much confidence we have, it is who we have confidence in that is important.

Question 4: If time is short, choose just a few of these verses. My favorites are: Psalm 119:90; Psalm 103:12; John 1:12–13; Titus 3:5; John 3:16, 36; and 1 John 5:10–13.

Question 6: In the original text, goodness and mercy are intertwined and are the godly attributes of lovingkindness and fidelity directed toward His creatures. It is the idea of steady support and kindness that one can count on from family members or faithful friends.

Question 7b: You may want to use Romans 5:8 "But God demonstrates his own love for in this: While we were still sinners, Christ died for us."

Question 8: Romans 8:28 gives New Testament insight into this question. "And we know that in all things God works for the good of those who love him, who have been called according to his purpose."

Question 9: Additional insight comes from Isaiah 55:8: "'For my thoughts are not your thoughts, neither are your ways my ways,' declares the Lord." We do not understand the Lord's ways, especially during difficult times. Corrie ten Boom used the illustration of a tapestry—when we look at the back side all we see are knots and broken pictures. But the other side of the tapestry reveals a beautiful picture. We won't see the entire tapestry of our lives until we look with heavenly eyes. Has the Lord revealed Himself enough to you that you can trust Him during the difficult times?

If Time Is Short
For an abbreviated lesson, concentrate on these questions in Chapter Seven: 3, 4, 6c, 7, 8, 9, 11, and 12.

Note from the Writers

We are just touching on the area of our future life with the Lord. We have tried to show throughout this book that David's Shepherd has further revealed Himself to us through the life of Jesus Christ. It is our hope that group participants have been able to see how faithful the Lord is to each generation.

Jesus was fully God and fully man, a mystery we cannot completely understand. He is our foundation, our Rock, and our connection with all that is eternal. David knew his Jehovah God, seeing Him as his Shepherd. David only had the first five books of the Old Testament, but his personal experience of the Lord was great. We have the entire Bible, with its New Testament fulfillment of prophecy concerning the Messiah.

How blessed we are to be able to understand our Creator and Redeemer so much more fully, through Christ's life, death, and resurrection! We can put our trust in Him and He will be faithful! We can look with confidence toward an eternity spent in the Lord's presence.

—Shelly Esser and Marcia Bueschel

Steps to Leading a Person to Christ

Before we can fully grasp the Lord as our Shepherd/Host, we must meet Him as Savior. If some members of your group have not yet discovered Jesus as their Savior, choose an appropriate time and place and use this brief outline to present the gospel message to them. Read through the Scripture verses carefully, answering any questions they may have.

Believe that God loves you so much that He sent His only Son, Jesus Christ, into our sin-sick world to become the Savior for our sins. See John 3:16 and Romans 5:8.

Agree that you are a sinner, separated from God by your sin, in need of His redemptive love and forgiveness. See Romans 3:23.

Agree that you must be born again if you desire to receive the new life Jesus died to give you, and that this can happen only through God's Holy Spirit. See John 3:5.

Repent of your self-centered life, lived independently from God, and receive His forgiveness. See Acts 3:19.

Accept Jesus Christ as Savior and Lord, as the payment for your sin and as the basis for your new life in Christ. Commit yourself to Him. He has already committed Himself to you! See John 1:12, Revelation 3:20, Ephesians 2:8–9, and John 3:1–8.

Pray to receive Christ right now through prayer (talking with God). Here is a sample prayer:

Lord Jesus, I need You. I have not known that You loved me enough to die for me. Thank You for forgiving me for my sin. I now welcome You into my life and desire to follow You. Amen.

Bibliography

- Baxter, J. Sidlow. *Explore the Book* (Grand Rapids: Zondervan, 1960).
- Briscoe, D. Stuart. *What Works When Life Doesn't* (Wheaton: Victor Books, 1977).
- Briscoe, Jill. *Overgrowing Evergreen* (Wheaton: Victor Books, 1986).
- Chambers, Oswald. *My Utmost for His Highest* (New York: Dodd, Mead & Co., 1966).
- Cowman, Mrs. Charles E. *Streams in the Desert* (Grand Rapids: Zondervan, 1965).
- Davis, John J. *The Perfect Shepherd* (Grand Rapids: Baker House, 1979).
- Griffith, Leonard. *God in Man's Experience* (Waco: Word Books, 1968).
- Jones, Mary Alice. *The Twenty-third Psalm* (Chicago: Rand McNally, 1950).
- Ketcham, Robert T. *I Shall Not Want* (Chicago: Moody Press, 1953).
- Keller, Phillip. *A Shepherd Looks at Psalm 23* (Grand Rapids: Zondervan, 1970).
- Kidner, Derek. *Psalm 1-72* (Downer's Grove: Intervarsity Press, 1973).
- Knight, George A.F. *Psalms Commentary* (Philadelphia: Westminster Press, 1982).
- Kunz, Marilyn & Schnell, Catherine. *Psalms and Proverbs* (Wheaton: Tyndale House, 1963).
- Leupold, H.C. *Exposition of The Psalms* (Grand Rapids: Baker Book House, 1969).
- Mayhall, Carol. *Filled to Overflowing* (Colorado Springs: NavPress, 1984).
- McGee, J. Vernon. *Commentary on Psalms* (Nashville: Thomas Nelson, 1991).
- Olson, Nathaniel. *The Lord Is My Shepherd* (Milwaukee: Ideals Publishing, 1978).
- Richards, Lawrence O. *The Teacher's Commentary* (Wheaton: Victor Books, 1988).
- Richmond, Gary. *All God's Creatures* (Dallas: Word Publishing, 1991).
- Slemming, C.W. *He Leadeth Me* (Fort Washington: Christian Literature Crusade, 1942).
- Stott, John. *Favorite Psalms.* (Chicago: Moody Press, 1988).
- Tenney, Merrill C. *The Zondervan Pictorial Bible Dictionary* (Grand Rapids: Zondervan, 1963).

Notes

Notes

Notes

Notes

Notes